END

In his powerful new book *The Joseph Calling*, Os Hillman illustrates that we are not designed without a purpose, that we have a larger story. Our purpose is not just what we do. Calling and anointing go together. Adversity builds Christlikeness. What will others say when your life is over? Os beautifully and intentionally shows that God develops character in his messengers through waiting, testing, and failure. Humility is the most important characteristic. From light to darkness, abuse to praise, isolation to temptation, pain and betrayal, all can lead to maturity as we learn to respond as Jesus did by maximizing our leadership as his creation. I heartily endorse this book.

—Tom Phillips, vice president,
Billy Graham Evangelistic Association;
executive director, Billy Graham Library

Os Hillman has a unique command of the revelation surrounding Joseph and his life. His mastery is the byproduct of a lifetime of research and personal experience combined with a special anointing to put it all together. Os can help you get accurate on fulfilling the call in your life. I love *The Joseph Calling* and heartily recommend it to you!

—Dr. Lance Wallnau, Lance Learning Group

Os Hillman has produced another excellent book, *The Joseph Calling*. I found the practical tools and personal anecdotes so encouraging and faith-building. What could be more important than discovering the reason God put us on this earth and how he equips us to fulfill it? This is a must-read for anyone who desires to be an instrument of transformation!

—Dr. Ed Silvoso, founder of Harvest Evangelism
and author of *Transform Our World*

The Joseph Calling is a rare jewel amidst a mountain of books on leadership. Within these pages, Os Hillman gives us an in-depth look at leadership from an angle of Scripture like we've never seen before. Eye-opening and right on target, this book is a must-read for any leader who not only needs a reminder of their purpose within God's bigger picture but also needs a map on how to get there.

—DAVID AND JASON BENHAM,
authors, *Whatever the Cost* and *Living Among Lions*

The Joseph Calling takes so many amazing principles that Os has taught over the years and puts the six stages into a concise reading with stories and insights that readers will be able to relate to their personal lives. Thank you, Os. What an encouragement you are to the people in the Kingdom of God!

—FORD TAYLOR, founder and president,
Transformational Leadership and FSH Consulting Group

Os Hillman has done it again with his informative new book *The Joseph Calling*. It is one of the most interesting and well written books I've been blessed to read in quite some time. He combines personal experience, which in some cases was devastating, Holy Scripture, the biblical history of mighty men and women called by God, and his own spiritual insight to help teach others about the significance of determining one's purpose and answering the question of why we were born. He also explains in detail how trials and tribulation build character and prepare us for accomplishing the purpose for which God created us. I highly recommend this book and am confident you will learn from it and hopefully be transformed by it.

—BOB WILLIAMSON, founder, chairman,
and CEO of the Jesus Alliance

I read in Os Hillman's *The Joseph Calling* that the core reason God created him was "to articulate and shepherd foundational ideas that lead to transformation." Well, Os has succeeded to do that here. Anyone desiring to live out the purpose God created you for and to understand how your disappointments, hurts, and pain fit into that purpose should read this book. It's rich with foundational biblical truths that will lead to transformation!

—KAREN COVELL, producer and founding director,
Hollywood Prayer Network

Os Hillman's extraordinary book is a treasure that will be a catalyst to anyone who desires to live an intentional and purposeful life. The six stages brilliantly weave personal, biblical, and practical experiences around a life-changing process that will fuel your passion to fulfill your destiny.

—STEVE FEDYSKI, COO, Pure Flix Entertainment

Though leadership books abound in numbers, Os Hillman's new book *The Joseph Calling* stands out with clarity. Os explains that the true leader is really God. And God takes people through stages that develop and transform them, not just for leadership, but for a life of deepest meaning.

—DR. DAVID BUTTS, president, Harvest Prayer Ministries

Os has once again found deep insight from Scripture on that seminal issue we each face: What is my purpose? What did God design me for when he brought me onto this earth? The closer we can take ourselves to this calling, the more vibrant and Spirit-led a life we will have. Join Os on that journey.

—PAT GELSINGER, CEO, VMware

In my journey, it seems to have always been life's challenges that have been used to shape my life. Now Os Hillman brings light to our struggles and their purposes in his new book *The Joseph Calling*. You will be encouraged as you read of fellow biblical sufferers.

—JOHNNY HUNT, senior pastor,
First Baptist Church, Woodstock, Georgia

The Joseph Calling offers a bright ray of hope for those in the midst of adversity as well as a biblical blueprint of what God may be doing in the midst of your difficulty.

—JIM LANGE, author of *Calming the Storm Within:
How to Find Peace in This Chaotic World*

Os Hillman brings great insight, depth, and understanding to the stages of preparation that God takes individuals through in order to maximize their potential and fulfill their greater purpose. Examples from leaders in the Bible as well as modern-day leaders will help anyone who reads *The Joseph Calling* to trust God's ways and processes, even through the dark times. A larger story is being written for each of us!

—NANCY ALCORN, founder and president,
Mercy Multiplied

In *The Joseph Calling*, Os Hillman gives us a solid biblical understanding of our process with the Lord. The fact that God has to work in us before we can manifest his Kingdom and fruit is a manifestation of his wisdom and his mark of quality assurance. Read the book, be inspired, and be a part of God's plan for restoration as a wonderful foretaste of a coming future.

—JAN STURESSON, international strategy advisor
and chairman of International Christian
Chamber of Commerce International Board

In today's world, most of us aren't worried about having food to eat or a place to sleep. But what we are seeking is a sense of purpose. We want to know why we are here on the earth. *The Joseph Calling* reminds us there is a ready guidebook that has shown story after story of how God uses real-life experiences to prepare us and to reveal to us our own Joseph calling. Recognizing these six stages in your own life will peal back the mystique and let you know with confidence why you were born.

—DAN MILLER, author and coach, 48Days.com

The writings of Os Hillman have been a source of encouragement, help, and blessing to hundreds of thousands of readers. His newest book, *The Joseph Calling*, will add to that list. I believe that many will be greatly helped by this book, including me.

—PAUL CEDAR, chairman and CEO,
Mission America Coalition

The Joseph Calling is a book that will bring hope and encouragement. Os Hillman has uncovered a pattern in the way God works with his people to produce godly people who fulfill their destiny. It is an easy read, brimming with examples from the Bible, from the author's own life, and from those around him. This book should be a reference for anyone who seeks to fulfill their purpose in life. I plan to teach it to my children and grandchildren.

—DAVE KAHLE, speaker, consultant,
and author of *The Good Book on Business*

Simplifying the complexities of this life journey is a rare gift. *The Joseph Calling* is a tangible expression of that rare gift. Os Hillman is a twenty-first-century scribe who has been gifted to communicate in writing the practical application of the truths many of us grapple with day to day. Well done, Os!

—PAUL L. CUNY, Marketplace Leadership International
and author of *Nehemiah People*

THE
JOSEPH
CALLING

6 STAGES TO DISCOVER,
NAVIGATE, AND FULFILL YOUR PURPOSE

OS
HILLMAN

BroadStreet

BroadStreet Publishing Group, LLC
Racine, Wisconsin, USA
BroadStreetPublishing.com

THE JOSEPH CALLING:
6 STAGES TO DISCOVER, NAVIGATE, AND FULFILL YOUR PURPOSE

Copyright © 2017 Os Hillman

ISBN-13: 978-1-4245-5472-0 (softcover)
ISBN-13: 978-1-4245-5473-7 (e-book)

Stock or custom editions of BroadStreet Publishing titles may be purchased in bulk for educational, business, ministry, fundraising, or sales promotional use. For information, please e-mail info@broadstreetpublishing.com.

Cover design by Chris Garborg/garborgdesign.com
Interior design and typeset by Katherine Lloyd/theDESKonline.com

Printed in the United States of America
17 18 19 20 21 5 4 3 2 1

To my two spiritual fathers who continue to
model the attributes of my heavenly Father:

J. Gunnar Olson
and
Jim Mezick

I called on the LORD in distress;
The LORD answered me and set me in a broad place.
The LORD is on my side;
I will not fear.
What can man do to me?
(Psalm 118:5–6 NKJV)

CONTENTS

Section Three
FULFILLING GOD'S CALL IN YOUR LIFE

FOREWORD

This is an important book because it deals with the difference between the attributed righteousness, which we received by faith in Jesus Christ, and the righteousness that comes from walking in obedience to God. Os Hillman addresses spiritual issues that sometimes are viewed as difficult or even contrary to the joy, liberty, and freedom we experienced when we first came to the Lord. This book is a treasure that needs to be read, reread, and digested many times over.

The kingdom of God is not mentioned in these pages all that much, and yet this book speaks about life in the kingdom of God. In God's plan of salvation, he purposed for the church to be an expression of the kingdom and to demonstrate the hope of the kingdom as it will come in its fullness. This involves the glorious experiences of the power of God. And it also involves the sharing of death to self in order for Christ to be revealed in us. As the Scripture says, "Christ in you, the hope of glory" (Colossians 1:27 NKJV). This process is often difficult and painful, but it is necessary and is a work of the Holy Spirit.

In *The Joseph Calling: 6 Stages to Discover, Navigate, and Fulfill Your Purpose*, Os Hillman has found a wonderful way of expressing these deeper things of the Lord. This book will cause many to mirror their own lives in the experiences he has shared and bring confirmation to their calling from God. This is of utmost importance as we all share in God's primary purpose—the coming of his kingdom, and that God's will is done on earth as it is in heaven—anything else would be to receive God's grace for selfish purposes.

—J. Gunnar Olson
Founder of ICCC,
International Christian Chamber of Commerce

A GOD-SIZED ASSIGNMENT

God is looking for his sons and daughters to be revealed in the world today. In fact, God has a purpose and destiny for each and every one of us. He has a God-sized assignment for each of us to fulfill on planet earth. But how does one know what that is, and how does God draw us into the larger story of our lives? Perhaps you've even wondered, can I know these things? The answer to this question is a resounding yes!

For more than twenty-five years, I've studied the ways of God and the processes by which he invites people into relationship with himself. More specifically, I've studied how God moves people into their specific calling. This has involved my own personal journey, which led me from a career as an ad agency owner in Atlanta to founding an international workplace ministry (which was not my idea) that has taken me to more than twenty-six countries (also not my idea) and allowed me to write seventeen books. And adversity was one of the key catalysts for this outcome.

This hasn't been simply an intellectual pursuit; it's my journey and the journey of many others I have discovered in the Bible, and in modern life, who were called by God to do something that made a significant kingdom impact for God. More often than not, the people God used were simply responding to a crisis event in their lives rather than initiating a vision that came from their own hearts.

Such was the case for Joseph. He was betrayed by his brothers, which led him through a thirteen-year journey of hardship, humble circumstances, accusations, time spent in prison, and much pain that resulted from wrongful judgments every time he turned around. But

God used his adversities to fulfill a larger story—or destiny, if you will—to be a spiritual and physical provider for the known world.

Most of us know God calls individuals into a specific assignment, but few of us know the processes by which he does it. The Joseph calling is a unique process that not all people will experience, but it is a verifiable process God takes people through to achieve a higher purpose for their lives. This process of discovery led me to discover six unique stages that Josephs must pass through in order to discover, navigate, and fulfill their destinies.

I have found that few people know their purpose and why God has put them on the earth in the first place. These are the issues I will address in this book—I want to help readers reconcile adversity and crisis with destiny and purpose. This book will reveal the six critical stages God's modern-day Josephs, almost without exception, experience in their destination toward the larger story of their lives. I've been able to document these stages in the lives of almost every major character in the Bible and in those whom God has used greatly in his kingdom in modern society.

When we understand God's processes, we're more likely to embrace his truths, and subsequently desire a deeper relationship with him. Welcome to the journey. I am confident you won't be the same person after you learn these six critical stages to fulfill your calling.

Ultimately, God is looking to make known his intention to use leaders to accomplish his plan on the earth today. Whether you're young or old, there's a plan of God for you at every stage of life. You will learn the signposts of his calling and how to respond to them. You will learn from the biblical stories and the modern-day case studies of those who have gone before us.

God wants to reveal to you your purpose, why he made you, and why he sent you into this world. He wants you to know his unique assignment for you—and only you—to fulfill on planet Earth. Are you ready to understand his process for fulfilling your larger story? Let's begin!

DISCOVERING
THE JOSEPH CALLING

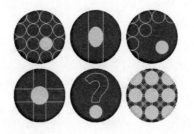

1

"YOU HAVE A JOSEPH CALLING ON YOUR LIFE"

> Nobody made a greater mistake than he who did nothing
> because he could do only a little.
> —Edmund Burke, Speech on Mr. Fox's East India Bill[1]

I n 1994 I was married, had built a successful ad agency for twelve
years in Atlanta, and had enough money in the bank to retire
comfortably. I led Bible studies, gave away money to Christian
causes, and thought I was a model Christian business leader. However, I was struggling in my marriage of fourteen years. We had
been in counseling most of our married life, and there were issues
I was constantly struggling with. Not only that, but I had a twelve-
year-old daughter who did not feel loved due to the marital con-
flicts at home.

In the spring of 1994, my world began to fall apart. My wife
wanted to separate. Within three months, several other things
began to happen: One day my investment manager called and said,
"It's all gone!" A Bernie Madoff scammer had confiscated half a
million dollars in investments and fled the country. Soon after,
my largest ad client, who represented 80 percent of our business,
refused to pay a $140,000 bill and fired us as their ad agency. And
just a short time later, my vice-president came to me and said he
was leaving the company. What he did not say was that he was taking my second largest account with him.

In three short months, my life shifted drastically—I would lose my family, my wealth, and my business. My wife divorced me and accused me of fabricating my losses to avoid a higher divorce settlement; I lost communication with my daughter for several months. Most psychologists say any one of those events is enough for the average person to commit suicide; I certainly felt as if life was over for me. The fact that I was a Christian only compounded the shame and guilt I felt from these failures.

I would struggle to make sense of my adversity for the next two years. Then one day a friend sent me an audiotape from a man named Gunnar Olson. On that tape, Gunnar talked about a "Joseph calling." He suggested that there are many who were going through adversity in their business and personal lives because of a calling that comes only from God. I had never heard of the concept of a Joseph calling before, and so I wanted to meet this man in person.

Gunnar was from Sweden. He was founder of the International Christian Chamber of Commerce, which operated in seventy-five countries at the time. He agreed to meet with me when he came to Washington for their international conference, which would be two months away. And so two months later I flew to Washington to meet with him. He was so gracious; he invited me to his suite and listened to my story.

After listening, he and his board member began to chuckle. I was taken back by their response to my crisis, but Gunnar quickly responded by saying, "Os, we are not trying to be rude. It's just that we have heard such similar stories from so many other marketplace leaders that it is uncanny to us. Os, you have a Joseph calling on your life." He then went on to explain, "A Joseph calling is a marketplace call that a man or woman goes through in order to become a spiritual and physical provider to others. You become known, just like Joseph became known, by the adversity you have gone through."

Gunnar then took out a napkin and drew a diagram. "This is where you are currently," he said. "As you begin to press into Jesus with all your heart, he will guide you to this next destination (spiritually speaking). You have probably made some mistakes during your process, but what you need to remember is your call is greater than the mistakes you have made. You have a marketplace call upon your life."

That day I walked into his hotel room as a shamed and defeated Christian businessman, but I walked out with an understanding that I was in the process of a call to the marketplace. That day Gunnar became my spiritual mentor and father. Now, twenty-five years later, I have spoken and ministered to men and women in the marketplace in twenty-six countries and written seventeen books, including a daily devotional that is read in more than a hundred nations (Today-GodIsFirst.com). God turned my Valley of Achor (trouble) into a door of hope for me and for many others (Hosea 2:15).

My crisis became my recruitment stage (stage one) that all Josephs go through. God would use the next seven years of my life as the character development phase of my journey. I would discover many things about the wounds of my past, generational strongholds that contributed to my marriage breakup, and character issues God was dealing with in order for me to become the man he wanted me to be.

During this time, God would send specific mentors to deal with particular issues he wanted to heal and correct in my life. At the end of the seven years, my character development stage, I was a different person—God had birthed a ministry. He healed my relationship with my daughter, and she joined me in our ministry. She has served with me almost eight years and has become a skilled writer and marketer (she has now pursued her own marketplace calling). God restored my finances—exactly seven years to the month of my crisis—and I became debt-free.

During those seven years, I also experienced stage three, which is the isolation stage. It was during that season where I began to write the daily devotional TGIF: Today God Is First. Each day for nine months, God would give me a Scripture verse and application for my adversity and marketplace calling. He showed me that many believers struggle to integrate their faith life into their work life. One particular verse that stayed with me during this time was Isaiah 45:3, which says: "I will give you hidden treasures, riches stored in secret places, so that you may know that I am the LORD, the God of Israel, who summons you by name."

> God often puts us through the experience and discipline of darkness to teach us to hear and obey him.

God was turning my mess into messages and me into a messenger. God often puts us through the experience and discipline of darkness to teach us to hear and obey him. We can then become his messengers as he births a message through our oftentimes painful life experiences.

Stage four is the cross stage, in which a leader is betrayed. For me, this came in the form of four major betrayals. Over time, all but one of those have been reconciled. But I had to learn the lessons Jesus taught about forgiving my enemies and washing the feet of Judas. I realized that unforgiveness was like living in a jail cell; in reality, forgiveness is more for us than for the other person.

Stage five is the problem-solving stage, which resulted in my being able to address the issue of bringing faith life into my work life and helping people understand their Joseph calling and the role adversity plays in each of our lives. Additionally, God has allowed me to be an international spokesperson on faith and work so I can sound a trumpet to call the nation back to God.

Through stage six, which is the network stage, I have developed my TGIF subscribers in 104 nations, and those who are members of our Change Agent Network. Additionally, God has made it possible for me to form key leadership relationships throughout the body of Christ to build unity for the sake of cultural transformation. He has burdened me with a call to John 17 unity in which Jesus calls us to be one as he and the Father are one—this is so the world might believe in him.

In summary, I have clearly seen the following six stages in my own life, the life of Joseph, and in the lives of other leaders God has significantly used in the kingdom of God. Here is a brief overview of the six stages that every person must go through in order to discover, navigate, and fulfill his or her purpose in life:

1. The recruitment stage. A crisis in my business led me to meeting Gunnar Olson in 1996 and a call to an international work life ministry.
2. The character development stage. Seven years of adversity became my years of character development. I had to pay off many debts over that period of time. However, God restored my finances at the end of the seven years and birthed an international ministry.
3. The isolation stage. During those seven years, I began to write. My messes became messages, and I became a messenger through my writing.
4. The cross. I had four major betrayals during this time particular stage, pushing me to learn the hard realities of forgiveness.
5. The problem-solving stage. I have been able to work with others in navigating their own seasons of adversity, help the body of Christ understand the role of faith and work, and be a catalyst for nation transformation.
6. The networking stage. My network has become my TGIF: Today God Is First subscribers, the Change Agent Network, and other leadership networks I collaborate with.

All believers must go through these stages in order to fulfill the call of God on their life. But if you are in a season of adversity right now, it is helpful to first discover your purpose and know why God has made you. Without that foundational understanding, the adversity and suffering won't be worth it. So let's delve deeper into what it means to discover your purpose and why God made you for such a time as this.

DISCOVERING
YOUR PURPOSE

The two most important days in your life are the day you are born and the day you find out why.

—Mark Twain[1]

I will never forget the first time a board member said to me, "Os, I think you know what your natural gifts and talents are, but I do not think you know why God made you." The truth is, I was taken back by that comment. I had heard people talk about purpose and destiny before, but why God made *me* had a little different meaning to it. Could one really know this anyway? I pursued her comment, and before I knew it we scheduled a full day for her to walk me through a simple process that has been beneficial to me, even to this day, twenty years later.

Later I discovered an unusual verse in Revelation that confirms this truth: "I will also give that person a white stone with a new name written on it, known only to the one who receives it" (Revelation 2:17). Each of us has a name in heaven that uniquely fits us and only us. However, before I get into this process with you, let's start where most people start—discovering God's purpose for one's life.

WHAT THE BIBLE SAYS ABOUT PURPOSE

The Bible says you were created and set apart by God: "Before I formed you in the womb I knew you, before you were born I set you apart" (Jeremiah 1:5). Not only that, but God created you and set you apart for a specific purpose: "'For I know the plans I have for you,' declares the LORD, 'plans to prosper you and not to harm you, plans to give you hope and a future'" (29:11).

God has preordained the works you are to do while you live on the earth. Paul wrote in Ephesians 2:10, "For we are God's handiwork, created in Christ Jesus to do good works, which God prepared in advance for us to do." If you are going to discover how God wants to use your life and work, then you must know why you were created in the first place. If you start trying to determine your purpose in life before discovering why you were created, then you will inevitably get hung up on the things you do as the basis for fulfillment in your life, which will only lead to frustration and disappointment.

> If you start trying to determine your purpose in life before discovering why you were created, then you will inevitably get hung up on the things you do as the basis for fulfillment in your life, which will only lead to frustration and disappointment.

Most people in society seek to find meaning and purpose from the following:

- Achievements: performance and achievement is where many find their ultimate value.
- Relationships: many people believe meaning in life is based upon the kind of relationships they have.
- Children: some believe purpose is found in having children or taking care of those children.
- Acquiring money and/or possessions: some people find meaning in acquiring money and material possessions.
- Recognition from others: some find meaning from what others think of them.
- Work/careers: some people derive their purpose and identity from their work/careers.

- Play hard: believe it or not, but some people believe they must work hard to be able to play, which is their ultimate goal in life.

No matter where you seek to find meaning and purpose, the truth is that without purpose life has no meaning at all. Isaiah tells us, "I have labored to no purpose; I have spent my strength in vain and for nothing" (Isaiah 49:4 NIV84). Most people lack purpose and meaning because they have no relationship with God. This is why the psalmist declared, "May He grant you according to your heart's desire, and fulfill all your purpose" (Psalm 20:4 NKJV). Finding your purpose begins with God and God alone: "Everything got started in him and finds its purpose in him" (Colossians 1:16 MSG).

God Chose You

First and foremost, God created you to know him and to have an intimate relationship with him. In fact, God says that if a person is going to boast about anything in life, then he should "boast about this: that they have the understanding to know me" (Jeremiah 9:24). The Bible encourages us to seek God first, which is why Jesus encouraged his disciples by saying, "But seek first his kingdom and his righteousness, and all these things will be given to you as well" (Matthew 6:33).

We know God chose us; he is the initiator and we simply respond to his invitation. This is why Jesus told his disciples, "You did not choose me, but I chose you and appointed you so that you might go and bear fruit—fruit that will last—and so whatever you ask in my name the Father will give you" (John 15:16).

Humankind's relationship with God was lost in the garden when Adam and Eve sinned. Jesus' death on the cross, however, allows this relationship to be restored and to have intimate fellowship with the Father once again. The apostle Paul came to understand this when he said, "I gave up all that inferior stuff so I could know Christ personally, experience his resurrection power, be a partner in his suffering, and go all the way with him to death itself" (Philippians 3:10 MSG).

Establishing this relationship with God is vital to discovering your purpose in life. If you don't have this relationship with God, then you will seek to fulfill your purpose out of wrong motives, such as fear, insecurity, pride, money, relationships, guilt, or unresolved anger. God's desire is for you to be motivated out of love for him and to desire to worship him in all that you do. As you develop this relationship with God, he will begin to reveal his purpose for your life.

Your purpose in life isn't something you decide to do; rather, it is chosen by God. It is nonnegotiable. God had a plan in mind when you became flesh and blood on earth. "The LORD will fulfill His purpose for me," the writer said (Psalm 138:8 MEV). There is no changing God's purpose for your life, but you may not fulfill it because free will is involved.

The Psalms tell us that we have an assigned portion (purpose and destiny). For example, David wrote, "LORD, you alone are my portion and my cup; you make my lot secure. The boundary lines have fallen for me in pleasant places; surely I have a delightful inheritance" (Psalm 16:5–6). The Bible even tells us that God even decided when we would live on earth and where we would live: "He marked out their appointed times in history and the boundaries of their lands" (Acts 17:26).

The Bible also says that "God's gifts and his call are irrevocable" (Romans 11:29). That is why someone can be a successful preacher and fall into sin and still have fruit from his or her preaching. Our gifts and callings are irrevocable. However, God will eventually deal with the sin of anyone who continues to misrepresent him.

Oswald Chambers explains another dimension of calling in *My Utmost for His Highest*:

We are inclined to forget the deeply spiritual and supernatural touch of God. If you are able to tell exactly where you were when you received the call of God and can explain all about it, I question whether you have truly been called. The call of God does not come like that; it is much more supernatural. The realization of the call in a person's life may come like a clap of thunder or it may dawn gradually. But however quickly or slowly this awareness comes, it is always accompanied with an undercurrent of the supernatural—something that is inexpressible and produces a "glow." At any moment the sudden awareness of this incalculable, supernatural, surprising call that has taken hold of your life may break through—"I chose you ..." (John 15:16). The call of God has nothing to do with salvation and sanctification. You are not called to preach the gospel because you are sanctified; the call to preach the gospel is infinitely different. Paul describes it as a compulsion that was placed upon him.

If you have ignored, and thereby removed, the great supernatural call of God in your life, take a review of your circumstances. See where you have put your own ideas of service or your particular abilities ahead of the call of God. Paul said, "[W]oe is me if I do not preach the gospel!" He had become aware of the call of God, and his compulsion to "preach the gospel" was so strong that nothing else was any longer even a competitor for his strength.

o———o———o *While you may not fulfill the purpose for which you were made, you still have a purpose that God intends for you to fulfill.* o———o———o

If a man or woman is called of God, it doesn't matter how difficult the circumstances may be. God orchestrates every force at work for His purpose in the end. If you will agree with God's purpose, He will bring not only your conscious level but also all the deeper levels of your life, which you yourself cannot reach, into perfect harmony.[2]

Your Purpose Is Not Always Tied to What You Do

While you may not fulfill the purpose for which you were made, you still *have a purpose* that God intends for you to fulfill. This is your blueprint from God. In the same way that he had a specific purpose in mind for Jesus when he sent him to the earth, so the Father has a specific purpose in mind for your life too.

This doesn't mean, however, that there is one highly specific niche for you to fill and that if you miss it then too bad. You can achieve your purpose in many different and creative ways. This should take the pressure off you in trying to find out what that one specific thing is that God wants you to do. You won't throw your entire life off course by choosing the wrong college, job, or mate. God is much bigger than any miscalculation or disobedience on your part. Isn't that comforting to know?

But defining your purpose will help you to determine the activities in which you should be involved. Jesus did not involve himself in activities that contradicted his purpose. His purpose was to do the will of the Father, and he never did anything contrary to that purpose. Jesus' specific assignment that was derived from his purpose was to defeat the work of the devil (1 John 3:8), to be the payment for the sins of humanity (John 3:16), to bring glory to his Father and do his will (5:30), and to bear witness to the truth (18:37).

In the same way, your purpose should always be to do the will of the Father. From your relationship with Jesus and the Father, you will derive your assignments that you are to do on earth. Oswald Chambers said, "Jesus never measured His life by how or where he was of the greatest use. God places His saints where they will bring the most glory to Him, and we are totally incapable of judging where that may be."[3]

Joining God in His Work

Several years ago, Henry Blackaby wrote a popular Bible study called *Experiencing God*, in which he described how one of the core principles is to join God where he is already working so that you find his purpose for your life.[4] When you involve yourself in activities contrary to this purpose, then you:

- begin to live a life of sweat and toil that leads to slavery instead of reaching the Promised Land of his rest.
- get off course from achieving the intended destiny for your life.
- produce dead works instead of the fruit of obedience rooted in your purpose.
- potentially lose your reward because you are involved in activity God never orchestrated.

Each of us must ask *why* we are involved in a specific activity. Is it a God activity, or just a good activity? Remember, Jesus only did something if he saw the Father doing it—and he could see what his Father was doing because of his intimate relationship with him.

Your Work Matters to God

In previous books, I have extensively covered the spiritual nature of our work from God's viewpoint. When Adam and Even sinned in the garden of Eden, the Bible says work became harder because the ground was cursed. Fellowship with God was broken. The planet was tainted by the sin of Adam and Eve. However, when Jesus paid the penalty of sin for Adam and Eve, and all humankind, he redeemed *all* that had been lost in the garden (Luke 19:10). That *all* includes our working life.

Our work is now to be worship to God. There is no sacred/secular divide when it comes to work. All of life is spiritual, which means we are serving the Lord Jesus Christ in and through our working life. This is why Paul wrote to the Colossians: "And whatever you do, do it heartily, as to the Lord and not to men, knowing that from the Lord you will receive the reward of the inheritance; for you serve the Lord Christ" (Colossians 3:23–24 NKJV).

We are to experience Jesus' life in and through our working lives. There is no hierarchy of spiritual vocations. A pastor is no more spiritual than the banker or the construction worker in the eyes of God. We are all in full-time Christian work; we just get our checks from different sources. The six stages of a Joseph calling are all designed to help us realize the larger story of our individual work life call.

DISCOVERING MY PURPOSE

I discovered my purpose later in life. I grew up thinking that my destiny was to be the next Jack Nicklaus. My dad started me playing golf when I was eleven years old. He encouraged me greatly in this area. I eventually became a good junior player, shooting under seventy several times before my fourteenth birthday and having three holes in one. I played in the 1967 US Junior Amateur in Boston, with several later-to-be-famous PGA golf professionals—Ben Crenshaw, Gary Koch, and Bruce Lietzke. I received a golf scholarship to the University of South Carolina. I was well on my way to becoming a professional golfer on the PGA Tour, but when I finished school and turned pro, I quickly grew frustrated and disillusioned with my inability to reach the level to play competitively as a professional.

Our family had always been a church-going family, but we knew little of the concept of walking in a personal relationship with God. However, when I was fourteen years old, my dad was killed in an airplane crash, which ultimately led my mom to a more intimate relationship with God. Through her influence and that of a pastor, I became a Christian in 1974.

As the years went by, I decided that golf was no longer the profession God wanted me to be in, so I made a career change into sales and marketing. But after being in various jobs for six years, I found myself longing to grow more in the Lord and serve him in a greater capacity.

I was involved in starting a church in North Carolina with two other men, which led me to begin thinking about whether or not I was really *sold out* for God. *Maybe I am called to be a pastor, and I should go to seminary*, I thought to myself. I took a leave of absence from my job and went to a three-month Bible study course at a retreat center in California. I moved to Atlanta to serve as an assistant pastor, only to have the position removed after three months. As one might guess, this caused me to go back into the business world. In hindsight, however, I see that all of this was the hand of God.

Through it all, I learned that I was never cut out to be a pastor or to have a *vocational ministry*; I was designed to be in the business world. However, I could not help but think of myself as a second-class Christian who was not quite sold out to the purposes of God. No one was saying this to me; it was more implied by the Christian culture around me. But I would later discover this was going to be a central focus of a call to the marketplace. In order to fulfill the Joseph calling on my life, I needed to know why God made me.

3

DO YOU KNOW
WHY GOD MADE YOU?

Life is 10 percent what happens to you and 90 percent
how you respond to it.

—Lou Holtz[1]

Coming to personally know God through Jesus Christ is the
most important step you can make toward discovering your
purpose in life. But once you know him, it is then important to
learn about your aptitudes, which helps to reveal your gifts, talents,
and passions. It also helps you understand your natural inclina-
tions.

In 2002, I met a woman by the name of Brenda who special-
ized in working with executives who were in career transition. She
had a keen understanding of how to help people discover their core
purpose in life from God's perspective; she challenged me to go
through this process. The goal at the end of the day was to create a
five-to-seven-word statement that defined my God-given purpose.
During this process, we identified my core strengths that most
represented me, such as teaching, networking, shepherding, communicating, and writing. All of these were attributes of my life.

Here are the core attributes I listed for my own life:

- Networker
- *Teacher*

- Athlete
- Marketer
- Planner
- Promoter
- Leader
- Communicator
- Organizer
- Golf instructor
- Father
- Mentor
- Sales/marketing positions
- Ad agency owner
- Vocational ministry
- *Articulator*
- *Shepherd* to others
- *Transformational* leader

Once we listed all of my characteristics, gifts, and talents, we then narrowed these down to the four that most represented me at my core (which are italicized above). My top four core characteristics are most representative of my DNA. We then wordsmithed these four attributes into a statement: "The core reason God created Os Hillman is to articulate and shepherd foundational ideas that lead to transformation."

> Understanding your unique gifts, talents, and passions helps you to better discover that purpose for which you were made.

The interesting thing is that my core purpose had been modeled even before my salvation, such as a teaching golf professional, a business consultant, and an advertising agency owner. I had articulated and shepherded ideas in each of these arenas. I could articulate and shepherd a person to be a better golfer or to run a better business. Today, God is doing this in a spiritual way through writing, mentoring, and leading a movement to help people understand their work as a calling that comes from God.

It is important that your statement be unique to you as a person and individual. It shouldn't be too generic. For instance, "God made me to love God and to love others" is too generic; this could be said of everyone. During one of my workshops, a woman came up to me and shared her statement: "I was made to glorify God in all I do." I said, "That is not your unique purpose. That could be said of everyone. Go back and focus on what is unique about you that is different from anyone else." Understanding your unique gifts, talents, and passions helps you to better discover that purpose for which you were made.

DIVINE CIRCUMSTANCES

Sometimes God uses divine circumstances to give a person a clue about his or her future. For example, even my unusual name—Os—turned out to be significant to the discovery of my purpose. You see, I am a third-generation business owner. My real name is Omar Smallwood Hillman III. Quite a mouthful. My parents put the O and the S together and called me Os. It is strange for someone growing up in the Southern United States to have a Middle Eastern name like Omar. But no one in my family knows the history of how I acquired that name; we only know that Smallwood was the name of the doctor who delivered my grandfather.

During my character development season, one of my mentors challenged me to find out more about the meaning of "Omar." My mentor sensed it had something to do with my future. At this time in my life, I was studying about the life of Esau and how he despised and discarded his birthright for a bowl of porridge. I was using this story as an analogy for those in the workplace who were discarding their birthrights for money and positions.

It was also during this time when I went away for a weekend to fast and pray. God spoke to me, telling me that I would "lead a marketplace movement." I had no idea what that meant at the time—I was a humbled and financially broke businessman. I had never written a book. Years later, however, this would be confirmed through others, even the national media. I would go on to write seventeen books and travel to twenty-six nations to teach men and women in the marketplace how to experience God in their working lives.

Throughout the Bible, we find that names were given as an indication of God's purpose for an individual. In some cases, names were altered to represent a significant change, as in Abram to Abraham, Jacob to Israel, or Sarai to Sarah. When I looked up the name "Omar," I discovered that it was Arabic for "first son" and "disciple," Hebrew for "gifted speaker," and German for "famous." In the Bible, Omar was a grandson of Esau (Genesis 36:15), and another meaning of his name is "eloquent."

These meanings related to my own life: I was the first and only son of my parents; I am a disciple of Jesus Christ; I felt God was calling me to public speaking. The puzzle pieces were coming together. God's preparation for my life would include becoming a steward of God's resources for his people in the workplace. Part of my job would be to help other descendants of Esau recover their birthrights, even though they may have traded them for earthly pleasure and prestige, or remained in Egypt as slaves and orphans instead of heading for the Promised Land.

To make sure that I was an instrument fully yielded to God's purposes, God took me through a seven-year season of character development where I experienced many painful losses. During this season, God allowed me to revisit earlier wounds in order to be healed and equipped for my future assignment. I am not the same man today I was in the '90s. God has delivered, healed, and matured me. What I overcame is now being used as payback to the enemy of my soul, who tried to use this process to steal, kill, and destroy my life. But now it is being used to free others from the same hindrances I had to overcome.

Someone once said, "God uses enlarged trials to produce enlarged saints so He can put them in enlarged places!"[2] Before the Israelites entered the Promised Land, they first had to pass through the desert. They had to trust God for their daily manna. The desert and character-developing season is only *a* stage in your life. When God has accomplished in you what he desires, then he will bring you out of that season. The Lord has given you a mission to fulfill that can only be fulfilled *after* you have spent an adequate amount of time of preparation in the desert.

> Don't fear the desert; it is there where you will hear God's voice as never before.

Don't fear the desert; it is there where you will hear God's voice as never before. The word *desert* in Hebrew means "to speak." It is in the desert where you will have the idols of your life revealed and removed, and where you will begin to experience the reality of a living God as never before. This is why God proclaimed through Hosea:

> Therefore I am now going to allure her;
>> I will lead her into the wilderness
>> and speak tenderly to her.
> There I will give her back her vineyards,
>> and will make the Valley of Achor (trouble)
>> a door of hope.
> There she will respond as in the days of her youth,
>> as in the day she came up out of Egypt.
> (Hosea 2:14–15)

DISCOVERING YOUR ANOINTING

In addition to discovering your purpose, you also need to discover the anointing that is on your life. We read about God's anointing in Scripture. The apostle John writes, "As for you, the anointing you received from him remains in you, and you do not need anyone to teach you. But as his anointing teaches you about all things and as that anointing is real, not counterfeit—just as it has taught you, remain in him" (1 John 2:27).

The anointing is a gift that functions easily when it is operating in you to the benefit of others and the kingdom of God. In his book *Anointing: Yesterday, Today, and Tomorrow,* R. T. Kendall explains it this way:

> The best way I have been able to describe [an anointing] is that it is when our gift functions easily. It comes with ease. It seems natural. No *working it up* is needed. It is either there or it isn't. If one has to work it up one has probably gone outside one's anointing. If one goes outside one's anointing the result is often fatigue—that is, weariness or spiritual lethargy that has been described as "dying inside."[3]

One area in which I have a God-given anointing is the area of networking. I have never sought to develop such an anointing, but I sure know a *lot* of people. Despite being an introvert, God has connected me with people all around the world. Many times, people call me about something, and my natural response is often, "Oh, you need to contact so and so about that. He can help you with that."

Where do you move naturally in your life? What do you do that you don't have to work at? Chances are, that is your anointing. God wants you to walk in the anointing he has given to you for his glory. This helps fulfill your God-given purpose.

BEING PROMOTED BEYOND YOUR ANOINTING

Discovering your anointing will also enable you to know when you are moving in a direction away from that which God has intended for your life. R. T. Kendall again explains how many believers often find themselves lured into accepting promotions and assignments outside of their anointing—a concept known as the Peter Principle:

> The way the Peter Principle works is this. A person who has been a first-rate typist or secretary may find themselves in management. As long as they were typing letters, taking dictation, or answering the telephone they were superb. They coped with ease. But a vacancy at a higher level came along and they applied for and got the job. They now have to make hard decisions, handle people under them, and find that they are under stress.
>
> They are not cut out for this after all—but try to stick it out. They have been promoted to the level at which they are not able to function with ease. They should have stayed with their old job. But no. They are determined to make it work. Few people will admit they have been promoted to the level of their incompetence.[4]

I have seen this principle in action over the years. In my own ministry, I have some key intercessors who support me personally. One time, I made the decision to put one of these individuals into the role of coordinating prayer for an event because she was an awesome intercessor who had a keen ability to hear God. However, I soon discovered that she was a poor networker and organizer. She was placed in a role in which her anointing did not lie. That was a good lesson for me.

God Works through Weakness instead of Your Natural Gift

Sometimes God manifests his presence through our weaknesses, and later they become our strengths. For example, I am not a natural public speaker. I am generally a shy and reserved person. In a group of people, I will usually be the one to speak the least. But when you give me a topic I am passionate about, such as helping people find God's call for their lives, I will talk your head off.

Because the message is more important than my comfort level, God empowered me to speak publicly about the message he placed in my heart. He has taught me how to be a speaker by trial and error.

> Sometimes God manifests his presence through our weaknesses, and later they become our strengths.

God often moves us beyond our natural gifting and allows us to receive through our obedience to him. Oswald Chambers provides some valuable insight regarding this. He wrote, "The call of God only becomes clear as we obey, never as we weigh the pros and cons and try to reason it out. The call is God's idea, not our idea, and only on looking back over the path of obedience do we realize what is the idea of God."[5]

God often has to get us into a position to accept a call from him. For many of us, this requires some sort of motivation for us to seek him. More often than not, this motivation comes through a calamity or crisis. When a crisis takes place in our lives, we begin to seek God for relief and answers. Over time, this process encourages us to seek God's face (in a personal relationship) instead of merely his hand of provision or a solution to our problem.

Most of us will have many experiences on our way to discovering the purpose for which God made us. For some of us, that destiny will not be an event or a specific experience, but a process that is played out over our lifetimes. However, although you may have a similar experience to mine, you also may be someone who starts out in the right place for your calling.

The apostle Paul made an interesting statement that indicates most of us will remain in the very jobs we were in when we came to know the Lord. He writes, "Usually a person should keep on with the work he was doing when God called him" (1 Corinthians 7:20

TLB). God has uniquely gifted you to perform a job in and through the workplace. And, in most cases, he wants you to remain in that place to fulfill his purposes through your workplace calling.

Many times, God uses mentors to help his sons and daughters in the path he desires us to take. Moses mentored Joshua, Paul mentored Timothy, Elijah mentored Elisha, and Jesus mentored the twelve disciples. I have had several mentors in my own journey and cannot tell you how important those mentors have been in my life.

AGE FOR CALLING AND PURPOSE

Calling and purpose are not always revealed at a certain age. The age of maturity was thirty in the Jewish culture. Joseph, Jesus, and David all began their core assignments at thirty years old, although God called them into their assignments when they were much younger. And Joseph and David went through their character-developing stage before they entered their assignment.

For David and Joseph, this was also their time of convergence. *Convergence* is when God's circumstances, your heart, your talent, your influence, and your social capital converge to maturity. But others got their assignment much later in life.

- Noah built the ark when he was five hundred years old.
- Abraham was initially called at seventy-five, and was a hundred when Isaac was born.
- Moses began his assignment when he was eighty.
- Joshua succeeded Moses at eighty years old and died when he was 110.
- John wrote Revelation in his nineties.

Others productively lived to extremely old ages: Methuselah, the oldest man recorded in the Bible, lived to age 969; Adam lived 930 years; and Enoch was 365 when he was taken to heaven.

BEWARE OF THE WELL-MEANING COUNSEL OF OTHERS

When God calls you to walk down a certain path, he gives you, and only you, the grace for that assignment. Do not let others sway you out of sympathy or reasoning. This is an important truth to embrace as you seek to discover the purpose for which God made you. Your calling is unique to *you*; do not compare yourself to others or listen to counsel based on natural reasoning alone.

Peter began to compare his circumstances to those of John. Then, just before ascending to the Father, there was an interesting conversation between Jesus and Peter about his future. John writes:

> Peter turned and saw that the disciple whom Jesus loved was following them. (This was the one who had leaned back against Jesus at the supper and had said, "Lord, who is going to betray you?") When Peter saw him, he asked, "Lord, what about him?"
>
> Jesus answered, "If I want him to remain alive until I return, what is that to you? You must follow me." Because of this, the rumor spread among the believers that this disciple would not die. But Jesus did not say that he would not die; he only said, "If I want him to remain alive until I return, what is that to you?" (John 21:20–23)

Now It's Your Turn

Discovering your purpose and why God made you are crucial to understanding God's processes in your life. The following exercise should be done with someone close to you who knows you very well. Spend time identifying your natural gifts and keep in mind which are the four most prominent. Once you complete your list, you will wordsmith them into a statement. You may want to come up with a few statements and see which one resonates with you and the person closest to you.

What Are Your Natural Gifts?
Step 1: Create your own list.

1. _____
2. _____
3. _____
4. _____
5. _____
6. _____
7. _____
8. _____
9. _____

Step 2: Narrow your list (choose four key words).

1. _____
2. _____
3. _____
4. _____

Step 3: Create your purpose statement (wordsmith it into a phrase).

_____
_____
_____
_____

PAUL POTTS: MOBILE PHONE SALESMAN

Several years ago, England's version of *American Idol* featured a contestant named Paul Potts. The chubby blue-collar-looking man with crooked teeth stepped onto the stage. The judges had already sized him up in their minds until a voice came out of that man that did not seem to fit. He sang opera like a seasoned professional. The audience cried in awe and excitement, and so did the judges. Even Simon Cowell said, "So you work at Car Phone Warehouse and you did that? I wasn't expecting that! You were fantastic!"

Paul went on to win the competition. He is now a famous opera singer. There is nothing wrong with being a mobile phone sales-man. However, Paul's larger story was the gift of singing. But life experience and lack of opportunity never allowed his gift to be dis-played. That is, until he was given the opportunity.

Your Life Is Multifaceted

Once you understand why God made you and discover his purpose and calling for your life, then you will realize God's call upon your life is multidimensional. Your life consists of your relationships with God, your family, your work, your community, your country, and your world.

Not everyone has a high-profile call, but we are all called. Some assignments are big and visible to others, while other calls might be hidden and seen by only a few. But be assured that God's reward is the same for both. It is all about fulfilling God's purpose for *you*. And it is vital that we understand that God works through the mundane and the ordinary as much as the more dramatic. "We are given to an incredible overestimation of the extraordinary at the expense of the ordinary," wrote Einar Billing.[6] And Oswald Cham-bers wrote:

> The things Jesus did were the most menial of everyday tasks, and this is an indication that it takes all of God's pow-er in me to accomplish even the most common tasks in His way. Can I use a towel as He did? Towels, dishes, sandals, and all the other ordinary things in our lives reveal what we are made of more quickly than anything else. It takes God Almighty Incarnate in us to do the most menial duty as it ought to be done.[7]

For many years I hosted a men's meeting at my home every other Tuesday night. I took all of the men through this process of discovering why God made them. Several men have come back to me months after we did this exercise and said, "That process has been the most impactful thing I have ever done in my life. It has helped me understand my wiring. I now know what not to do and what I should be doing."

Your Epitaph

We all need to live our life for an audience of one. We need to fulfill God's purpose for our lives. Once you identify your purpose, it is helpful to write the epitaph of your life. What might others say if you fulfilled your complete purpose on earth once you are gone? What would you write on your own tombstone? I hope mine will say, "His adversities helped many."

4

DISCOVERING THE JOSEPH CALLING

We must accept finite disappointment, but never lose infinite hope.

—Martin Luther King Jr.[1]

Once we discover our purpose and why God made us, then the six stages of the Joseph calling have more meaning for discovering, navigating, and fulfilling our purpose on earth. But what is the Joseph calling? How can we define it? The Joseph calling is a marketplace call that is marked by those who have gone through adversity, which has led them to become a spiritual and physical provider to others.

When we think of Joseph, we often think of the adversity he went through to achieve his ultimate destiny. He had a unique marketplace call upon his life that was earmarked by extraordinary adversity, which, in turn, was used to save a nation from starvation and usher him into his eighty-one-year assignment to be second in command in Egypt. He was betrayed by his brothers and wrongfully accused of raping Potiphar's wife, causing him to be thrown into prison—this brought a total disruption to his life. The Joseph calling is a unique calling that not every leader has; those who have it are known for the adversity they are required to go through in order to fulfill a special assignment from God for their lives.

This calling begins with a dream. At the time of Joseph's dream, he was an immature teen who more than got under the skin of his older brothers. He evidently had a big mouth that got him into trouble. Joseph was also a pet son of his father, Jacob, which further infuriated his brothers. His dream revealed that he would stand over his brothers one day and even his father would come before him and bow down.

Joseph told his dream to his brothers; and they hated him even more. So he said to them, "Please hear this dream which I have dreamed: There we were, binding sheaves in the field. Then behold, my sheaf arose and also stood upright; and indeed your sheaves stood all around and bowed down to my sheaf."

And his brothers said to him, "Shall you indeed reign over us? Or shall you indeed have dominion over us?" So they hated him even more for his dreams and for his words.

Then he dreamed still another dream and told it to his brothers, and said, "Look, I have dreamed another dream. And this time, the sun, the moon, and the eleven stars bowed down to me."

So he told it to his father and his brothers; and his father rebuked him and said to him, "What is this dream that you have dreamed? Shall your mother and I and your brothers indeed come to bow down to the earth before you?" And his brothers envied him, but his father kept the matter in mind. (Genesis 37:5–11 NKJV)

God took Joseph through a time of personal transformation that involved extraordinary levels of pain and disappointment in order to bring him low before he could be brought high in the kingdom realm. That process involved being betrayed by his own family, sold as a slave, and being wrongfully accused for a sexual crime he did not do; he completely lost his reputation but was faithful in using his God-given gifts to serve others while in prison.

The six stages of this process are designed to bring us to a place where God can fully trust us with all he wants to do in our lives. He knows he can trust us when we can glorify him in the process of the pain and suffering. If we fail to do this in our pit, then we will fail to glorify him in the elevation period. The truth is that if we walk away from God because of something bad that happens to us, then we never really had a relationship with him in the first place.

> God releases his blessing in proportion to the character you allow him to develop within you.

God's goal is to make us servants, stewards, and slaves. And so the adversity period in our lives is designed to remove our dependence upon titles and accomplishments for our self-esteem. God brings us to the place where all we want is Christ in us in order to create Christ in others. That is when we know the testing has accomplished its purpose.

God releases his blessing in proportion to the character you allow him to develop within you. He will totally ruin you and remake you at the same time. The result of this will be a new you, where you will be grateful to God for what he had done within you. Someday you will be able to say that you would actually go through the process again if it meant you would gain what you gained.

God turns the pit into a well of the Holy Spirit—he makes a deposit that will last a lifetime. The psalmist reminds us, "As they pass through the Valley of Baka ["trouble"], they make it a place of springs; the autumn rains also cover it with pools" (Psalm 84:6). This journey through the Valley of Baka is designed to help us become sons and daughters of the living God.

Joseph Was a Type of Christ in the Old Testament

Jesus ("The Lord saves.")	Joseph ("Increase; he will add.")
• Operated in the supernatural through signs and wonders. • Was sinless. • Provided salvation for humankind. • Suffered for and forgave those he was sent to save. • Betrayed by his own people, the Jews, and was sold for thirty pieces of silver. • Served as a physical and spiritual provider. • Gave prophetic words: he foretold things to come. • Operated in the marketplace. • "The government shall be upon his shoulder" (Isaiah 9:6 KJV).	• Operated in the supernatural through dreams and words of wisdom. • His hardship was not due to sin. • Saved a nation from starvation. • Suffered for and forgave those he was sent to save. • Betrayed by his own family was sold for twenty shekels of silver. • Served as a physical and spiritual provider. • Gave prophetic words: he foretold things to come. • Operated in the marketplace. • "The government shall be upon his shoulder" (Isaiah 9:6 KJV).

GOD OF THE VALLEY

There is a scripture in 1 Kings that helps us understand what it means to glean from the valley experience: "The man of God came up and told the king of Israel, 'This is what the Lord says: "Because the Arameans think the Lord is a god of the hills and not a god of the valleys, I will deliver this vast army into your hands, and you will know that I am the Lord."'" (1 Kings 20:28). The Arameans were wrong—God *is* the God of the valleys too.

Whenever we stand on the mountain, we can see clearly. It is the best vantage point to see what lies ahead. Wouldn't it be great to live on the mountain all the time so that we could always anticipate what is ahead? God allows us to experience the mountaintop at times. Joseph's first mountaintop experience was as a young man. He had the favor of his father; he was given a fine coat and even had a dream about his future.

As a young man, Joseph had a sense of his destiny. God often gives us a picture of our future so that we will remember this picture when we are being tested. This is so that we can trust him in the valleys. However, this usually doesn't reveal how God intends to bring about his purpose in our lives.

It is important to understand that none of us really derive the character qualities God desires for our lives while we are on the mountain. It is in the valley where the fruit is planted and harvested. Fruit cannot grow on the mountain; it must grow in the valley. God is a God of the mountains, but he is even more a God of the valleys.

In the valley, it is more difficult to see ahead; the clouds often cover the valley and limit our sight. Joseph was thrust into a deep valley that left him wondering if the God of his fathers had forsaken him. Jesus hoped that he might be able to avoid the valley that caused him to sweat drops of blood, hoping there would be another way besides going to the cross. There is a valley that each of us must enter, usually unwillingly, in order to experience the God of the valley—and to experience his faithfulness in the valleys.

Once we have spent time in the valley, we come out with something we would have never gained if we had not entered it in the first place. The valley brings much fruit into our lives so that we might plant seeds into the lives of others. God does not waste valley experiences. If we are faithful in the valley, then we will enter a new dimension with God that we never thought possible. There is a harvest of wisdom and virtue that can only be grown in the valley.

The apostle Paul understood this process when he wrote:

We are troubled on every side, yet not distressed; we are perplexed, but not in despair; persecuted, but not forsaken;

cast down, but not destroyed; always bearing about in the body the dying of the Lord Jesus, that the life also of Jesus might be made manifest in our body. For we which live are always delivered unto death for Jesus' sake, that the life also of Jesus might be made manifest in our mortal flesh. So then death worketh in us, but life in you. (2 Corinthians 4:8–12 KJV)

AVOIDING SELF-DELIVERANCE

It is important that we do not extricate ourselves out of our valley experience. If you advance yourself before it is time, then it will result in leanness in your soul. Our timetable for advancement out of the valley is dependent on our obedience in the valley. God doesn't measure timetables; he measures growth. The Israelites were supposed to enter the Promised Land in only twelve days. However, their disobedience kept them in the desert for forty years!

> God doesn't measure timetables; he measures growth.

Read the psalmist's description of this time in Israel's life:

> I am the LORD your God,
> Who brought you out of the land of Egypt;
> Open your mouth wide, and I will fill it.
> But My people would not heed My voice,
> And Israel would have none of Me.
> So I gave them over to their own stubborn heart,
> To walk in their own counsels.
> Oh, that My people would listen to Me,
> That Israel would walk in My ways!
> I would soon subdue their enemies,
> And turn My hand against their adversaries.
> (Psalm 81:10–14 NKJV)

God's bigger plan for Joseph would be revealed later as described in Psalm 105. God revealed the level of testing that would be required of Joseph:

> Moreover He called for a famine in the land;
> He destroyed all the provision of bread.
> He sent a man before them—
> Joseph—who was sold as a slave.
> They hurt his feet with fetters,
> He was laid in irons.
> Until the time that his word came to pass,
> The word of the Lord tested him.
> The king sent and released him,
> The ruler of the people let him go free.
> He made him lord of his house,
> And ruler of all his possessions,
> To bind his princes at his pleasure,
> And teach his elders wisdom.
> (Psalm 105:16–22 NKJV)

Joseph would have to pass four major tests in his life: the test of betrayal and forgiveness, the sexual temptation test, the perseverance test, and the stewardship test. He would pass each of these tests, which qualified him for the elevation God would give him at thirty years old. God always takes you down before he takes you up. He allows you to be forsaken in order to usher you into a deeper relationship with himself. You must have the acclaim of God before you have the acclaim of people. By the time you go through this process, you will not care a bit about the acclaim of others. That's the purpose for the training ground—to remove all trust in yourself and your abilities.

We are in a season of Joseph preparation for many of God's chosen leaders. These are unique times we live in today, in which God is shaking the foundations of every nation on the earth. We need to better understand the role God is calling each of us to play in the days ahead.

A Swiss Businessman Models the Joseph Calling

I first met Juerg Opprecht at the 1995 Global Consultation on World Evangelization (GCOWE) conference that had over four thousand attendees from over seventy-five nations that had come to Pretoria, South Africa. Gunnar Olson was the director of the marketplace track and it was there I met Juerg for the first time, though only briefly. Over the next several years, both Juerg and myself would bump into one another at conferences. And we both went through our own Joseph pit experiences.

I recall visiting Juerg in the early 2000s after attending a marketplace conference in Germany. I decided to drive to Bern, Switzerland, and visit with Juerg and his wife, Benzli, in their well-appointed home on a lake in the valley of the Swiss Alps. It was during this time I told Juerg I felt something was different about him—he had a different spirit about him. He said he felt the same about me. We were both on the other side of our major Joseph pit periods.

> God always takes you down before he takes you up. He allows you to be forsaken in order to usher you into a deeper relationship with himself. You must have the acclaim of God before you have the acclaim of people.

He began to open up his heart about some of the challenges God had been taking him through. There were personal challenges in his family and the family business that had taken him to a place of brokenness. He had sold the family business and invested his money in an IT enterprise that would later fail, becoming his pit experience. We both shared our common experiences and about what God taught us and how we had changed as a result.

I began to hear of the fruit that was coming from his life after successfully walking through that season of adversity. It was during that season that God began birthing things through Juerg that reflected his heart to be a blessing to people, communities, and nations.

Business Professionals Network

The desire to work as an entrepreneur for the growth of God's kingdom continued to occupy Juerg's thoughts. In 1997, he was invited to speak at a workshop in Bishkek, Kyrgyzstan, on the topic of how to construct a business. This was five short years after the fall of the political Soviet Union and the fall of the planned economy system. The people had been forced to change from a planned economy to a free market economy from one day to the next. Impossible! The many ministers he encountered complained that their greatest challenge was the unemployment rate of more than 60 percent.

Juerg was moved by God when he heard this. The next night he awoke and read Matthew 25:35–36, but instead of the way it actually read, he saw a new ending: "For I had no work and you found it for me." And, as Jesus says in verse 40, "Truly I tell you, whatever you did for one of the least of these brothers and sisters of mine, you did for me."

He recognized the voice of God and promised to help the workshop participants. He did not yet know how he was going to do that, but he trusted God's voice and knew that God would guide him in finding a way. That was the birth of the Business Professionals Network (BPN), which has since supported and encouraged 880 entrepreneurs in five developing countries and thus helped to create or sustain more than fifteen thousand jobs. BPN works to provide not only a livelihood for entrepreneurs and their families but also an ability to retain their own dignity.

A Joseph in His Community

Juerg had the opportunity to allow his diverse interests and talents to unfold and support others on their personal journeys. He began to invest in other areas as well. Inspired by Oswald J. Smith's book *The Passion for Souls* and with great assistance from a minister friend of his, Juerg decided to build two Christian community centers in central Bern, Switzerland, complete with church halls, restaurants, offices, and living accommodations. He also invested in apartment buildings and industrial and manufacturing properties. The revenues from these and other investments were used to support his social and Christian commitments.

My last visit with Juerg was in 2014 when I had a ministry trip to Switzerland. I stayed in his home with him and his wife, and I had a wonderful opportunity to experience another entrepreneurial venture of Juerg's.

Several years earlier, Juerg was able to fulfill a childhood dream. This new venture became the source of much fanfare in Lenk, Switzerland, a resort community. In order to rescue the dilapidated Lenkerhof Hotel, he spent six months developing a new concept for the hotel and one and a half years realizing it and renovating it.

In December of 2002, the new Lenkerhof Gourmet Spa Resort located in the Swiss Alps held its grand opening, serving young wealthy clients across Europe. It proved to be an immediate success with reservations booked months in advance. In 2005, the Lenkerhof was chosen as the Swiss Gault Millau Hotel of the Year. I had the privilege to tour the hotel and have lunch with Juerg and Benzli as they shared their incredible hotel with me.

In 2012, the hotel celebrated its ten-year anniversary, proving that the values used in reinventing it had also proven to be the groundwork for its success. Hotel director Jan Stiller praised it as he recalled the previous ten years: "It was touching to watch as both guests and employees were moved to tears as Juerg Opprecht's vision was born into a reality in the hotel. Juerg Opprecht's values came alive in the re-creation of the Lenkerhof."

Though the first ten years had been successful, the financial crisis in 2007 had taken its toll on both Juerg's investment and his nerves, but his long-term vision paid off. He weathered the storm as God sustained him through this difficult downturn in the world economy. Benzli also plays a major role in ensuring the hotel models a different spirit, focusing on giving five-star level services to its clients. She even declared the noble resort a "fear-free zone." She said, "Our employees are free to discuss any concerns they may have as long as they maintain a respectful approach."

Hotel directors Jan Stiller and Heike Schmidt experienced this firsthand: "We were going through a difficult time and came to the Opprechts for help. They invited us into their home and talked openly and honestly with us. The emotional support they gave us let us know that we were not just another employee to them. Their open arms policy gave us strength and warmth and helped us through this difficult time."

Juerg Opprecht is an example of a Joseph in the marketplace. God took him through his season of preparation for greater use in the kingdom by using his entrepreneurial gifting to bless people, communities, and even nations. Like Joseph, Juerg became a spiritual and physical provider for others. He understands what it means to walk in the Joseph calling.

5

THE PURPOSE
OF THE JOSEPH PROCESS

Leaders lose their right to selfishness. It means giving up
personal options in order to guide the people to where
they need to go.

—John Maxwell[1]

When Joshua, the priests, and the people of Israel were to
cross over the Jordan, there were twelve men who had to go
before the Jordan was parted. They had to wade through the deep
water and the mud in the Jordan to find the precious stones that
would be used as a memorial of this special day. It was the hardship
and mud-drenched lives of the twelve who paved the way for the
miracle of the parting of the water in the Jordan for the presence of
God (the ark) and the people to cross over on dry ground.

Josephs are those who go through the mud to get to where
God is calling them. They may feel like they have lost everything
at times, and they may have in the natural, yet God promises to
protect them in the midst of their adversity. Joseph prospered, but it
was a different kind of prospering amid going through the furnace
of affliction. The book of Genesis tells us, "The keeper of the prison
paid no attention to anything that was in Joseph's charge, because
the LORD was with him; and whatever he did, the LORD made to
prosper" (Genesis 39:23 ESV).

In this process of discovering, navigating, and fulfilling our purpose in life, we may find ourselves in situations or required to do work we never wanted to do, yet God gives us favor even in that place. This is true for many modern-day Josephs who are displaced from their past careers due to the economic climate in which we live, but they realize God's favor is with them in the "prison" in which they find themselves. There may be destruction all around us, but God will preserve our lives. Malachi confirms this when he prophesies:

> "For behold, the day is coming,
> Burning like an oven,
> and all the proud, yes, all who do wickedly will be stubble.
> And the day which is coming shall burn them up,"
> Says the LORD of hosts.
> "That will leave them neither root nor branch.
> *But to you who fear My name*
> *The Sun of Righteousness shall arise*
> *With healing in His wings;*
> *And you shall go out*
> *And grow fat like stall-fed calves.*
> You shall trample the wicked,
> For they shall be ashes under the soles of your feet,
> On the day that I do this,"
> Says the LORD of hosts.
> (Malachi 4:1–3 NKJV, emphasis mine)

Like the twelve men who had to go across the Jordan before Joshua, who got wet and muddy, those who are given the Joseph calling must endure hardship so that many others who will come behind may enter their spiritual Promised Land. This is the special calling for God's Josephs. It may involve betrayal just as Joseph and Jesus experienced; it may require losing all your earthly possessions; it may even require losing relationships dear to you. But you must be able to say as Joseph said, "You meant evil against me, but God meant it for good" (Genesis 50:20 ESV). Why? "So that I would be sent ahead for your benefit and others coming behind me." God tells us that *all* things will work together for good in the end (Romans 8:28).

It is worth noting here that those who bought Joseph from his brothers were Ishmaelites. These were the descendants of Ishmael, who came from Abraham's sin when he took plans into his own hands, deciding to help God fulfill the vision to have a son who would be heir to the family. With encouragement from Sarah, he slept with his maidservant Hagar. This error in judgment directly impacted the nation of Israel, as well as the world.

However, God has a way of checkmating the devil. He uses satan's miscalculation and preserves a nation through Joseph. God is always one step ahead of the devil's plans—and even our own plans. No matter how bad you have blown it in your life, God *can* make something good out of it. Jesus is the only person who made plan A, but for the rest of us, God turns our plan B and C into his plan A.

GOING DEEP IN THE MUD

The Joseph process is a circumcision and baptism procedure that is personal, painful, and bloody. It is messy, but it is also necessary. God is picky with his leaders. He almost killed Moses because he refused to circumcise his child after eighty years of preparation. Moses prepared for forty years in Egypt, being educated and trained, learning the ways of the nation he would have to relate to forty years later; then he spent another forty years tending sheep and being alone in the fields (isolation). All of this was preparing Moses for his assignment.

Then God came to him and told him to take off his shoes (he was on holy ground) and lay down his staff (Moses would perform miracles with his staff). That staff was representative of Moses' vocation as a shepherd. God was saying that he was going to use Moses' lowly position as a shepherd, a vocation viewed as the lowliest by an Egyptian, to perform miracles. And miracles he did!

God used Moses to perform ten miraculous plagues, bring water from a rock, create the Ten Commandments, and part the Red Sea to name only a few. Like Moses, we all must come to a death in ourselves before we are resurrected into the call of God. There is a purpose in this death process. However, death without resurrection is only defeat. God does not want you to remain in this place; he has plans for you once you have gone through the valley phase.

WHEN THE POWER COMES

It was not until Jesus sent out his disciples that the power of God was released through them. He gave them hard instructions when he sent them out without money or clothing, beyond what was on their backs: "Then Jesus asked them, 'When I sent you without purse, bag or sandals, did you lack anything?' 'Nothing,' they answered" (Luke 22:35).

Jesus requires total dependence on him for our every need. It is that dependence that creates a spiritual environment for power and miracles. And the same will be true for his Josephs as God takes them through their preparation time. It is not enough to teach people or be taught; they must also be engaged in the battle.

When the disciples went out the first time, they were amazed that even the demons responded to them. There is always a trumpet call that requires a leader to step into the larger story where he or she can experience the power of God. It is here where expansion takes place. It is here where the power of God is experienced. Knowledge without experience is fruitless. This is a condition of the modern church today—knowledge without power. We are full of knowledge but many are never engaged in the battle. The body of Christ needs to recognize we are in a war for the souls of people and for the future of our nations.

RICHES IN THE MUD

Our world may be torn apart and our losses in the material world may be significant, but there are great riches we gain from the Joseph process that will be used in our lives and in the lives of others. We need to be grateful that God considers us worthy for the assignment. We "mud-dwellers" have had to endure for the sake of others coming behind us. A mentor once said to me, "It is important you get through this incredible season of hardship; there are many depending on you to get through this!" At the time, it seemed like a strange statement. Who was I that others would be depending on me to get through my stuff? But now it all makes sense.

Here is the story of the twelve men crossing over the Jordan before the rest of the Israelites:

> Then Joshua called the twelve men whom he had appointed from the children of Israel, one man from every tribe; and Joshua said to them: "Cross over before the ark of the LORD your God into the midst of the Jordan, and each one of you take up a stone on his shoulder, according to the number of the tribes of the children of Israel, that this may be a sign among you when your children ask in time to come, saying, 'What do these stones mean to you?' Then you shall answer them that the waters of the Jordan were cut off before the ark of the covenant of the LORD; when it crossed over the Jordan, the waters of the Jordan were cut off. And these

stones shall be for a memorial to the children of Israel forever." (Joshua 4:4–7 NKJV)

Crossing the Jordan is symbolic of a form of baptism for the Joseph leader, a baptism of the mud of God. These leaders will be used to lead others into the Promised Land. This is why the psalmist could write, "As they pass through the Valley of Baka, they make it a place of springs; the autumn rains also cover it with pools" (Psalm 84:6).

Many have benefitted from the lessons I have learned through my own trials. God takes us through the valley of weeping so we can drink of the springs that make spiritual deposits in us and refresh us from one spiritual spring to the next. These deposits become our anointing to free others from slavery and to bring heaven to earth.

What we overcome becomes our payback to the enemy of our souls for his attacks upon us, and it becomes our anointing and authority to free others. It is what we learn in the valley of trouble that will be used to establish his kingdom on earth: "I will give her vineyards from there, and the Valley of Achor as a door of hope; she shall sing there, as in the days of her youth, as in the day when she came up from the land of Egypt" (Hosea 2:15 NKJV).

Every leader God used discovered there was a time and moment that was a turning point in his or her life:

- Moses met God at the burning bush.
- Noah received instructions to build the ark.
- Gideon was called to destroy the idols.
- Esther was called to save the nation.
- Paul was called to preach to the Gentiles.
- Peter called to lead the church.

Each person was an answer to something God had in mind for what he wanted to do on the earth. The question must be asked: What has God reserved you for? We need to understand the trigger that sounds the trumpet to our assignments from God, and we need to respond regardless of our financial means. Jesus did not call large organizations that were well funded; he called individuals and imparted an anointing on their individual lives to manifest the kingdom through them for each situation in which they found themselves. Jesus provides resources for the assignment to which each of us are called. When people see the power manifested in our midst, then God will use it to invite others in.

What is going on in your world, or *the* world? You and I are called to come with the answer to the problem. Jesus always solved a problem in the life of the person he met. This is where the power was manifested, and this is how we gain influence in the world today. It is a by-product of a relationship with a living God.

If we only teach people, then we will have people indebted to us, and bonded to us, but they may never be engaged to do anything. There must be a prophetic dimension to each of our calls. That means we must be aware of the events that become the trumpet call, which invites us into the larger story where the power of God is released in our lives.

We cannot be just a club of Christians. It must be more than that. Faith without works is dead. The Word became flesh and dwelt among us to manifest the kingdom of God in every area of life. The apostle Paul expressed this truth when he said, "And my speech and my preaching were not with persuasive words of human wisdom, but in demonstration of the Spirit and of power, that your faith should not be in the wisdom of men but in the power of God" (1 Corinthians 2:4–5 NKJV).

THE FAITHFULNESS OF ISAAC

Not everybody is a Joseph—some are called to pick up where the previous leader laid a foundation. Such was the life of Isaac. He was called to carry out the original vision given to his father Abraham. His test came when there was a famine in the land and God told him not to go to Egypt, but to depend on God for his provision in the place where he was. When everyone was fleeing to Egypt, he had to stay the course and not do what seemed logical or expedient at the time. He had to believe God.

> There was a famine in the land, besides the first famine that was in the days of Abraham. And Isaac went to Abimelech king of the Philistines, in Gerar.
>
> Then the LORD appeared to him and said: "Do not go down to Egypt; live in the land of which I shall tell you. Dwell in this land, and I will be with you and bless you; for to you and your descendants I give all these lands, and I will perform the oath which I swore to Abraham your father. And I will make your descendants multiply as the stars of heaven; I will give to your descendants all these lands; and in your seed all the nations of the earth shall be blessed; because Abraham obeyed My voice and kept My charge, My commandments, My statutes, and My laws."
>
> So Isaac dwelt in Gerar. ...
>
> Then Isaac sowed in that land, and reaped in the same year a hundredfold; and the LORD blessed him. The man began to prosper, and continued prospering until he became very prosperous; for he had possessions of flocks and possessions of herds and a great number of servants. (Genesis 26:1–6, 12–14 NKJV)

Many Josephs may find themselves in a famine, wanting to jump ship to solve their lack of provision during their testing. But we must hear God for direction as to how he wants to provide for our needs during this time. It is often the season where we are living on manna, just as the Israelites had to live on God's daily provision. He is Jehovah Jireh in every situation. If we jump ship when he has not instructed us, this could thwart the plans of God.

JESUS MENTORED THE TWELVE

The feeding of the five thousand was a mentoring case study in which Jesus showed the disciples what the power of God they would experience in the future looked like. When Peter walked on the water, it was a mentoring moment. When Peter got instructions on how to catch more fish and get his taxes paid by getting a coin from a fish's mouth, these were all mentoring moments. The disciples were learning to manifest the presence of God in the area of their calling.

We are living in an exciting time. It is a time where darkness is getting darker and light is getting lighter. It is a time for manifesting God's kingdom on the earth. Jesus prayed for heaven to be manifested on earth. How are you going to do that? "For the earnest expectation of the creation eagerly waits for the revealing of the sons of God" (Romans 8:19 NKJV). There is a purpose to the process of the Joseph calling—God will use the six stages of the Joseph calling to help us discover, navigate, and fulfill the destiny God has for each one of us.

6
—

LIVING SUCCESSFULLY THROUGH YOUR JOSEPH CALLING

There are those who look at things the way they are, and ask why. ... I dream of things that never were, and ask why not?
—Robert Kennedy[1]

Before we enter the first stage of the Joseph calling, the crisis stage, there is often a dream or vision of what we believe God may be calling us to do. Joseph had a dream that indicated something was going to happen in his future. He did not totally understand his dream, but that dream had a devastating impact on his life when he publicly shared it with his brothers, who demonstrated that they could not handle it.

Joseph was immature and lacked wisdom at this stage of his life. His brothers perceived him as the favored son at their expense—he got a beautiful coat the others did not get, and so his brothers became jealous of Joseph's favoritism. His dream was from God, but his handling of it showed an immaturity that God was going to use to create a new Joseph and save a nation through him. God used this dream to usher him into the crisis stage.

DEATH OF A VISION
Often our initial vision must go through a death process before it can become God's vision. God's vision begins its first stage through

a crisis. For Joseph, it was being thrown into a pit to be sold as a slave. This would lead him into his character-building season, which is the second stage, that would last for thirteen long years. His original vision had to die in order for it to be fulfilled.

Abraham had to realize that Ishmael was not the promised son. God had a different way to create a nation through Abraham and Sarah that would require a supernatural solution, not a natural one. The disciples had to die to the dream that Jesus was going to be a leader of a political movement. His death caused a crisis and confusion in the disciples. They did not understand the death of Jesus until he came back to life and revealed to them his purpose that would become their purpose.

We all start out with dreams for what we believe life should be like. We grow up thinking about being successful, getting married, having children, and having a "wonderful life." In the classic Christmas movie *It's a Wonderful Life*, George Bailey knew what he wanted in life. He did not want to stay in the tiny town of Bedford Falls and run his father's local savings and loan company. Losing his depositor's money through someone who would steal his money never entered his life's plan. But it happened.

> Often our initial vision must go through a death process before it can become God's vision.

It was a classic Joseph story with a wonderful redemptive ending that revealed to George Bailey something that he could not see for himself. His crisis forced him to see things he could not see without the crisis. His community and the people around him dearly loved him. Bedford Falls was where his calling was to be lived and experienced. He was to become a provider to his community. He was a Joseph.

Oswald Chambers explains the test this way: "God's method always seems to be vision first and then reality. So many mistake the vision for the reality, but in between the vision and the reality there is often a deep valley of humiliation. ... How often has a faithful soul plunged into a like darkness; after the vision has come the test and the darkness."[2]

In 1996 I started a magazine called *Christians in Business*. I thought this was my promised son. But it wasn't. It was my Ishmael that came with another major debt obligation and more frustration. I would later learn that the promised son was TGIF: Today God Is First, a daily devotional that was birthed out of a life experience, not something I thought of in the natural. It has become a lifeline for hundreds of thousands of people in more than a hundred countries, and it became the central thing that launched me into a worldwide ministry.

When Joseph was thrown into the pit, it ushered in a crisis that must have created a level of fear Joseph had never known before. He was thrust from one place in life to a whole new place, with no rights or choices, and, no doubt, with a questioning of God's love. "Where is my God? How could he let this happen to me? What happened to the dream I received from God?"

We all question God when bad things happen to us: "What did I do wrong that this could happen to *me*?" But make no mistake about it—this is a natural response to calamities. But we cannot remain there. We must remember that we live in a war zone. Satan wants to steal, kill, and destroy our lives, but Jesus says he came to give us life abundantly (John 10:10). God's goal for our lives is Christlikeness more than our own comfort. He has no problem allowing us to go through some times of discomfort if it means we will become more Christlike.

The Black Hole

There is a time within the crisis stage that all Josephs experience, which I call the black hole. It usually comes in the first phase of your crisis. The black hole is a time when all of life is disrupted and you have no ability to do anything about it. You may lose your finances or your health or even your job. Life is kicked out from under you. It is like being thrown into a rowboat with no oars and the boat has small holes in it. You are simply waiting for the boat to fill up with water and you fear you will go down with it. Sometimes what you fear comes to pass, but other times God takes you through a process that reveals his activity in your circumstances and provides for you in a supernatural way.

This stage is the best and worst of times. It is the worst for obvious reasons, but it is also the best because you begin to see the activity of God show up in the most unusual ways. You have a heightened sense of his activity in your life after the initial black hole stage. Oswald Chambers gives us some insight in times when we see only nothingness all around us:

> Whenever God gives a vision to a Christian, it is as if He puts him in "the shadow of His hand" (Isaiah 49:2). The saint's duty is to be still and listen. There is a "darkness" that comes from too much light—that is the time to listen. The story of Abram and Hagar in Genesis 16 is an excellent example of listening to so-called good advice during a time of darkness, rather than waiting for God to send the light. When God gives you a vision and darkness follows, wait. God will bring the vision He has given you to reality in your life if you will wait on His timing. Never try to help God fulfill His word. Abram went through thirteen years of silence, but in those years all of his self-sufficiency was destroyed. He grew past the point of relying on his own common sense. Those years of silence were a time of discipline, not a period of God's displeasure.[3]

GOD'S DOUBLE-TALK

Another aspect of the black hole is God's seeming sabotage of your ability to complete the task during this season. Nothing is more frustrating than carrying out a task and having your superior thwart your efforts to do what he or she asked you to do. Moses must have felt this way after God told him to go to Pharaoh and tell him to release the people of Israel. He said, "I am going to give you the power to release the children of Israel by the miracles I will do through you." Yet at the same time, he told Moses they would not be released because he was going to put a hard heart in Pharaoh: "The LORD said to Moses, 'When you return to Egypt, see that you perform before Pharaoh all the wonders I have given you the power to do. But I will harden his heart so that he will not let the people go'" (Exodus 4:21).

How do we reconcile this?

In my own life, I knew God called me to certain endeavors, yet every time I turned around a roadblock stood in my way. It took years of plodding along before the light came on as to why there was such a distance between what God called me to do and the manifestation of that calling. When David was anointed king of Israel, it was years before he realized the manifestation of that calling. There are a number of reasons for these types of delays.

In the case of Moses and Israel, God wanted to demonstrate his power in such a way that generations would be able to hear the story of their deliverance from their ancestors. God wanted greater glory from the situation; he also wanted to deal with Egypt by sending specific plagues. Finally, the process built character in Moses and tested him to see if he would stay the course.

There is a time for everything. If God has called you to some endeavor and you are frustrated that it has not manifested yet, know that times of preparation and simmering are required before the vision can be achieved. Seldom does God call and manifest the vision at the same time. There is preparation. There is testing. There is relationship building that must take place between you and God. You will only see this vision materialize once the process is complete.

ISOLATION

Stage three often leads us into isolation. Joseph was isolated from his family and all that he knew. This stage can also be described as the desert stage. When the Israelites were freed from slavery, they had to pass through the desert. Hosea 2:14 tells us, "Therefore I am now going to allure her; I will lead her into the wilderness and speak tenderly to her."

The desert is a place where God speaks. In fact, God gets you alone with himself, where you have no comforts and you are forced to live on manna alone. You cannot earn a living for yourself; you are totally dependent upon God. Your comforts are removed—you might even lose your car or your mobility.

I have four friends who have gone through their Joseph process. Two of them lost their cars for a season; two of them lost their homes. Those kinds of losses can be devastating for a man. Our pride is wounded deeply. It makes us feel like failures, especially if we have children and a wife for whom to care. When we lose our ability to care and provide for those we love, it touches us at the core of our beings. But we must realize that God is doing a deep work in our souls if he allows us to experience this.

One of my friends who went through this process was a successful real estate entrepreneur and national speaker on investing in real estate. He was a traveling speaker for one-day events and was on the same program with Donald Trump in cities across the nation. He made hundreds of thousands of dollars a night. When the real estate bubble broke, however, his career and finances crashed—he lost his home, his wife left him, and he lost his car. It was a humbling time in his life. However, God began to remake this man and has done a deep work in his character. He is a different man today than the one I first met.

God has given him a new vision and has birthed a new company through him. He has written a book and developed a relationship with God that motivates him to spend hours and hours with God. His story is still birthing, but I can see God maturing his vision and I expect that God will raise him up again to be a major influence in business and the kingdom of God.

> Sometimes the winds of adversity force us to adjust our sails to capture a different kind of wind.

Friend, you may feel like you are in prison; you may feel stuck in your circumstances. Let God meet you in this place. Let this be a time of discovering the power and presence of God during adverse circumstances. Sometimes the winds of adversity force us to adjust our sails to capture a different kind of wind.

Extraordinary afflictions are not always the punishment of extraordinary sins but are sometimes the trials resulting from God's extraordinary gifts. God uses many sharp-cutting instruments, and polishes His jewels with files that are rough. And those saints He especially loves, and desires to make shine the most brilliantly, will often feel His tools upon them.[4]

Joseph was one of those servants in whom God allowed adversity in order to save a nation. Jean-Pierre de Caussade said that when our pain is blinding and our dreams shatter, we can't move ahead in our own light, because we have none. We move forward only in the light of faith.[5] And Bruce Wilkinson said, "When God is pruning you, you hurt somewhere in particular. The pain comes from the point where His shears are snipping something away."[6]

God has used adversity to prepare many of his leaders for an earthly assignment. Part of this process is designed to loosen our grip on the cares and influence of this world. C. S. Lewis once said, "If I find in myself a desire which no experience in this world can satisfy, the most probable explanation is that I was made for another world."[7]

"It's a Ghost!"

When the disciples saw Jesus walking on the water, their first response was, "It's a ghost!" (Matthew 14:26). However, Jesus revealed that it was him, and then he invited Peter to get out of the boat and walk on the water (v. 29). What began as an event that created great fear in the disciples became a miracle of a man supernaturally walking on water.

God is doing a deep work in your soul during the crisis stage, the character-building stage, and the isolation stage. He is creating a nature change in your soul. What you value begins to shift; you will no longer care about what you once cared for. You begin to appreciate the simple things in life. Relationships become more important and God strips you of those character traits that hindered you in your past. He uses this time to bring healing to areas that need healing.

God delivered me from a stronghold of insecurity and fear during this season. I was a supercontroller, rooted in fear and insecurity. I could not trust God for my finances. But God used the crisis stage to take me into a wound that began in my childhood and manifested this behavior in me. He took me through a time of healing and deliverance. I am no longer the man I was before the crisis. Paul tells us that each of us is called to a transformed inner life: "And do not be conformed to this world, but be transformed by the renewing of your mind, that you may prove what is that good and acceptable and perfect will of God" (Romans 12:2 NKJV).

Sometimes people ask me how long God will leave them in their desert. I often say, "You will remain in the desert until it does not matter to you anymore." When Joseph was brought out of the prison and elevated to second in command in Egypt, I don't think it mattered that much to him. He was a "dead man" by this time—God had already done the deeper work in his heart. He was at peace with God and his circumstances. That is often when things begin to change.

Joseph's stage four, the cross, occurs on the front end of his crisis.

In fact, it becomes the catalyst for all the other stages that take place in his life. Our six stages are not always in sequence. Joseph would have to work through his betrayal for many years before he could personally forgive his brothers for what they did to him.

THE PROBLEM-SOLVING STAGE

Stage five is the problem-solving stage. Joseph would enter his problem-solving stage with each new assignment. First, it began in serving as a slave in Potiphar's household. Potiphar appreciated the gifts Joseph had, so much so that he gave him total reign over the household affairs. Potiphar's wife wanted Joseph to have sex with her, but he refused, so she accused him of rape. That refusal got him thrown into prison because Potiphar could not side with Joseph, no matter how much he knew his wife was a liar.

Joseph used his gifts in prison to serve the prison guards and became known for his administrative gifts. The more faithful we are at using our gifts in serving others, the more God will begin to elevate us. We need to be faithful in the small areas where our serving has little benefit to us personally. It's when we have been faithful over time that God honors that faithfulness.

Joseph served the cupbearer by giving him an interpretation of his dream. This was the seed that would lead to his freedom, but he had no idea at the time. Joseph was simply serving others with his gift. He hoped that it might make a difference when he asked the cupbearer to remember him when he was freed.

> The more faithful we are at using our gifts in serving others, the more God will begin to elevate us.

God supernaturally allows a problem to surface at a national scale for which Joseph had the answer. Pharaoh had a dream and Joseph had the solution. When it is time for you to come out of your desert season, it will come when there is an opportunity for you to be the solution to a problem. And God will use you to solve the problem. For some this comes in the form of a new business idea, while for others it comes as an opportunity to solve a problem for your employer.

This solution becomes your authority from which you minister to others. God framed what I do today by what I learned during my desert season. He birthed a message and a solution to issues I would later share with others. I could have never imagined myself doing what I am doing today. God turned a shy, poor student who barely got out of English class into an international author and speaker. Only God does stuff like that. He turns our weaknesses into his strength once he deals with the core issues of our lives.

I have a friend who was a leader of a national ministry. He and his wife have experienced incredible pain from the loss of two adult children through unusual accidents. It took years for the wife to get to a place of peace with God. I ran into this friend at a conference some time ago and asked how they were doing. He said, "The most amazing thing happened. My wife had been struggling greatly with the loss of our daughter. Then one day, God met my wife in her bedroom. He revealed himself to her in the most amazing way. It changed her. She is no longer the same person she was. This has now led us to start a ministry to those who lost family or friends in accidents." The truth is that we all need an encounter with God along the way; it is the only thing that will sustain us and heal us.

This is often how God works. He is not always the source of the calamity, but he will use it if we allow him to heal us and do the deeper work in us. Satan is often the author of the pain designed to kill us. However, Paul tells us that God makes all things work together for good for those who love him and are called according to his purposes (Romans 8:28).

There is no failure or calamity that happens in our lives for which God cannot make something good come out of it. It may never bring back a loved one or change a circumstance, but there will be a redemptive aspect to the situation if we allow God to do the work in us.

THE RESURRECTION

God supernaturally brought Joseph into proximity to Pharaoh for Joseph to solve the problem Pharaoh had. This happened because Joseph was obedient in using his gifts while he was in prison. He could have been so bitter that he refused to serve others; but instead, he used his God-given gifts in whatever circumstance he found himself in. However, because he used his gifts to serve others, those who would ultimately be the catalysts to deliver him from prison knew of his gifts and became his advocate and promoter. This is an important truth: Sometimes God wants to see if we will serve others amid our own pain; this becomes a source of healing for others and the catalyst that leads to our own freedom.

Through Joseph's pit experience, God gave him favor with his captors, which would ultimately be the reason for his elevation. When we use our gifts, God becomes our PR representative.

I have a friend who was displaced from his career due to the mortgage crisis in America. He had to shut down his business he operated for thirty years. He was forced to take a ten-dollar-an-hour job. It was not long before the employer saw his incredible work ethic and how he handled customers. His employer saw his attention to detail and soon elevated him. He is not yet making the same money as he made in his former business, but he is going through a season of preparation. God will restore that which "the locusts have eaten" (Joel 2:25). It takes time for the story of God to develop in each of our lives.

There is another man I have been working with who has a similar story. This man had a career in professional golf. He was a self-professed womanizer; he was also a heavy drinker. He was always the life of the party, and it was nothing for him to go out one night and come home with a woman. I first met this man at the golf course where I play.

Seeing where he was in his life, I began to see that God was beginning to work in his life. He lost his job and his home. He had already lost his three wives to divorce years earlier; he was now a single man in his fifties without kids, wondering how he got to this place. This caused some introspection that led him to open his heart to spiritual truths.

Since God was beginning to work, I began to reach out to him. As we spent time together, I spoke into his life. He responded with questions and started attending church once again. One day I invited him to attend my Tuesday night men's group. What he heard and experienced in that group changed his life. He felt cared for by our men and God ministered to him personally every time he came.

God is building a new nature in my friend; the man I see today compared to the man I first met are not remotely close to the same person. It is wonderful to see the work of God in an individual. God delivered him from his playboy lifestyle and placed him in another head pro job, strangely enough, through my connections.

There is another man in my group who has been separated from his wife for eight years. Hearing his story and the personality of his wife and how she has treated him would make almost every person I know say, "Why bother? Cut your losses and go on!" However, this was not his response. He has a deep conviction about the covenant of marriage that has been a testimony to all of us in the group. He has often had trouble holding a steady job that covers his expenses and child support. There have been times when we have prayed for his situation. Even though his wife seems cruel sometimes, my friend stays the course. Recently he came up to me after the group and said, "My situation has been improving. My wife is allowing me to spend time with her and my daughter. God has shown me things about myself that has helped reframe my attitude toward my wife."

Wow! What a turnaround after eight years of separation! It is still a work in progress, but where there has been no progress for eight years, we are now seeing fruit from his obedience and perseverance.

God is going to use this man's testimony in the lives of many others as he stands in the gap for his marriage. God is looking for real men, men who are willing to die for the sake of their wives and their children. This death can be the hardest. It is a death to our comforts, our conveniences, and our rights as men and husbands. In order to love your wife as Christ loves the church, it will require a death.

New Life, New Career, New Values, and a New Nature

Joseph was elevated to the number two position in the land; only Pharaoh had greater power than Joseph. He had access to wealth, although he himself may not have been wealthy, which is another attribute of Josephs. They will always have influence, but they may not necessarily be personally wealthy. Relational capital is sometimes as important as financial capital.

Joseph's thirteen years of slavery and imprisonment led to an eighty-one-year assignment from God to be second in command in Egypt. His final stage would be his networks of his eleven brothers. These eleven brothers would become a nation, God's chosen nation. Would you be willing to go through a thirteen-year training program for an eighty-one-year career that had incredible power, influence, and lifestyle? Oswald Chambers tells us, "If you have received a ministry from the Lord Jesus, you will know that the need is never the call: the need is the opportunity. The call is loyalty to the ministry you received when you were in real touch with Him."[8]

Your situation may not lead to such an extraordinary outcome, but what you can be sure of is there will be a nature change in you as a person. You will have new values reflected because of the deeper work God has done in your life. There will be new opportunities to which to respond. Chances are good that God will create something out of your crisis that you cannot have ever imagined would even be possible.

I am still amazed at what has come out of my seven years in the pit. There are losses that never got restored that still have a place of heartache in me. But the sting is no longer a day-to-day thing. There has been healing. Hebrews tells us that not everyone got that for which they were trusting God; some had to wait until the life after to receive full compensation for their life of faith and obedience: "These all died in faith, not having received the promises, but having seen them afar off were assured of them, embraced them and confessed that they were strangers and pilgrims on the earth" (Hebrews 11:13 NKJV).

I am no longer my own—I was bought for a price: "I have been crucified with Christ; it is no longer I who live, but Christ lives in me; and the life which I now live in the flesh I live by faith in the Son of God, who loved me and gave Himself for me" (Galatians 2:20 NKJV). I have discovered that I needed to look at life through a different lens. Peter wrote:

> In this you greatly rejoice, though now for a little while, if need be, you have been grieved by various trials, that the genuineness of your faith, being much more precious than gold that perishes, though it is tested by fire, may be found to praise, honor, and glory at the revelation of Jesus Christ, whom having not seen you love. Though now you do not see Him, yet believing, you rejoice with joy inexpressible and full of glory, receiving the end of your faith—the salvation of your souls. (1 Peter 1:6–9 NKJV)

We all must trust God for the things we cannot understand or resolve in our human understanding. There are questions of why we will not be able to resolve them until we meet Jesus in heaven. He will have a good answer then, but for now I can leave the questions with him. He can make it known to me if I need to know. One of the things Paul never did was ask the why question. He had plenty of reasons to question God for the extreme hardships he experienced, but he had a greater understanding of God and his love than his need to reconcile his hardships. Paul wrote, "For now we see in a mirror, dimly, but then face to face. Now I know in part, but then I shall know just as I also am known" (1 Corinthians 13:12 NKJV).

THE JOURNEY
OF A "JOSEPHINE"

You must retain faith that you will prevail in the end, and
you must also confront the most brutal facts of your cur‑
rent reality.

—Admiral Jim Stockdale, prisoner of war
for eight years in Vietnam[1]

D enise D. Campbell is a successful advertising executive from
Chicago who has two master's degrees. Life was good in 2007.
She gave her life to the Lord in November of that same year. She had
a six‑figure income and was heading up the ladder of success as a
media sales executive. But that all changed in July of 2008 when the
recession hit.

She was laid off from her job, which ushered her into a sev‑
en‑year season of adversity. Over the next several years, she would
be thrust into the greatest time of adversity of her life. Denise lost
all material evidences that reflected the success she had experi‑
enced in her career. She lost her Mercedes, her home of thirty‑eight
years, and, as she learned to explain it, "all my earthly possessions
had been removed, all that I obtained without him ... from my life.
My life had been emptied of all that was Egypt!"

When I met Denise, she was in her seventh year of that season
and had not held a job since 2008. Her isolation was so loud and
the separation from all that was formerly her life was so painful that

she was brought to tears on many sleepless nights. There were times when she wondered if God had abandoned her—she was experiencing her "black hole." She told me:

I could not get a job even though I had great interviews. People would fly me into town for an interview and I would think it went great, but I was never offered the job. Opportunities would appear and it would seem that I was only waiting on the start date, yet they would mysteriously disappear … as if the process itself was just a part of something I had only imagined. It was truly miraculous, in a negative way. I could not get a $29,000 job! I even tried to get a job at Niemen Marcus as a salesperson and couldn't get hired. Some people would often respond, "You are overqualified." I tried to work anywhere.

The seven years after 2008 were a process of God teaching me to walk with him and learn to live on manna. I have seen the activity of God in my life like never before. God has been changing me from the inside out over these years.

In May of 2014, I was awakened from my sleep and God told me to go and pray. While praying, he began to reveal himself to me and said, "You have a Joseph calling on your life for this generation." I had never heard of a Joseph calling. I began to do research on the Internet and your picture on the website came up. I watched your video with you talking about the Joseph calling. You said you had been in the ad business and your story began to sound strangely similar to my story. I was glued to your video! I too had been in the advertising business, so all of this seemed crazy and was relating to me personally.

I studied your website for months, and I felt the Lord was saying, "You need to speak to Os." I did not know how to get a hold of you, yet that morning was somehow different. The still small voice of the Holy Spirit spoke to me. He said to simply call the number on the website, so I did.

On December 14, 2014, I called you, seven months after I was awakened and told by the Lord I was a Joseph. I left a voicemail message, and to my shock you returned my call on the same Saturday I called, not long after I left a message. I screamed when you returned my call. You sent me your article on the Joseph calling and that article was describing me. You encouraged me to read your book *Upside of Adversity*.

I ordered it and devoured it; it really spoke to me. It was my story! Your book reflects my pain, my life, and my journey. I can't talk to anyone about this process. You are the only one who understands this process. God removed many relationships from my life in 2010 and 2011 for my benefit, I would realize later. "Why do I have to be so poor?" I complained to God. God said, "You are not poor, you are rich. There is a vision coming forth." Meanwhile, I ran out of unemployment.

I went through my black hole that you speak about in your book. You said, "One cannot even punch yourself out of a paper bag when they are in the 'black hole.'" I have experienced the black hole phase of the journey as you call it; it is the nightmare that seemed like it was never going to end. I realized your book spoke right into my situation. It was a catharsis of my life!

I had to be in Atlanta a short time later for a wedding and you were gracious to come meet me for coffee. During this amazing and difficult season, God had been using sevens in my life, which is his number of completion and perfection. He first revealed seven to me through a supernatural encounter with the Holy Spirit. While at the laundromat, as I spent seven dollars for a wash cycle, he miraculously

replaced it in my hand! To confirm that it was him, he presented another seven dollars inside my purse as he instructed me to look inside! I have been in this season seven years.
I met you at seven o'clock on January 7th! It's been crazy!

I find that people do not understand this Joseph process.
They tell you all sorts of things and try to counsel you on
what you should do and not do, and they question you as to
why you do not have a job. Even well-meaning family members and close friends try to encourage you to find something out of your core area just to put food on the table.

God began to reshape my thinking and strategically orchestrated a life-altering meeting with my pastor. It was the
beginning of my journey to gain an understanding of faith
and work. I attend a twenty-four-thousand-member church
in Chicago, and my pastor spoke into my life that set my
feet on the path leading into this "faith in the marketplace"
world. He requested to meet with me and said he believed
God wanted me to study the Bible and its application to the
marketplace. He said to me, "There is a need for God to be
integrated into every area of life, including business. There
is something you are to do around that."

I did not understand what he was saying; it sounded
Greek to me! I asked him if he had a prototype that I could
research. He didn't. He believed it by the Spirit of God, and
he said that it was inside of me. He said, "I want you to research kingdom principles in the marketplace and get back
to me." At the time of my initial meeting with my pastor, I
had absolutely no clue what he was talking about. I began
doing research on this. Years before this, God gave me a title for my business card, Visionary Agent of Change, which
I had been using, and, of course, I had no knowledge of
your book *Change Agent*. Being obedient to my pastor's instructions, I moved forward. Even though I did not know

what I was looking for, I started researching faith-based companies.

During this time, God began to manifest healing miracles through me. I would pray for people and they would report back to me that they had been healed. I used to yearn for my old life and my old friends, but God changed my heart about all of that. I would question God and asked him where had all the people—family and friends—gone? He answered me, "They have not gone anywhere. I have removed them for my purposes!"

I am now impacting the kingdom of God in ways I never thought possible. To be used as a vessel, as a conduit of God's miracle-working power, is a joy that is unexplainable. This process was necessary to be re-created for his use. It has been the best and worst of times. I am still in my process, but I see the vision from afar. I don't know where God is leading, but I know the one who is leading. And I take comfort in that.

Denise is an articulate woman, and I can see God working in her life. She was embracing the process, which is not always the case. She is going deeper with God, something every person God uses must do to see his or her process manifest the call on his or her life.

God gave Denise tremendous experiences of learning to trust and be led by the Holy Spirit. He was teaching her about his economy of provision in a desert season. He was, like Joseph in prison, manifesting supernatural gifts of healing and discernment for others. The Bible says God prospered Joseph while he was in prison. God was prospering Denise in her "prison," and someday she will be called out to have greater influence in the marketplace. It is our job to wait for the deliverance.

Denise is no longer the person she was in 2008. She has been transformed and equipped by this process to do the work of the kingdom. She has come to a place of trusting God daily and looking forward to the next stage of her Joseph journey.

WHY WE GO THROUGH ADVERSITY

Let me make some observations about why many of us go through adversity. There are three reasons for adversity: First, we reap what we sow. If we have been living a life with the values of Egypt, with sweat, toil, manipulation, and striving, then we will eventually reap the consequences of what we sow.

Second, we can experience warfare over our destinies. Jesus said that satan seeks to steal, kill, and destroy our lives. In the case of Joseph, it is my belief that satan entered the heart of his brothers to try and destroy him. However, God had purposes for Joseph and he preserved him, yet he did not deliver him for thirteen years. These are the ways of God that are not easily understood.

> God desires good things for his kids, and he will always take what the devil means for evil in our lives and turn it around for his glory.

In the case of Denise, this describes her journey. It was not God who took these things away; it was the enemy of her soul. God desires good things for his kids, and he will always take what the devil means for evil in our lives and turn it around for his glory. Paul tells us, "And we know that all things work together for good to those who love God, to those who are the called according to His purpose" (Romans 8:28 NKJV). As Denise turned to God in her trials, God has met her and is making something good out of it for his purposes.

The third reason we experience adversity is simply to experience the reproof of God as sons and daughters. This type of reproof is more of a process by which God deposits something into us that may involve adversity for our benefit. It also gives us evidence that we are sons and daughters of our heavenly Father:

If you endure chastening, God deals with you as with sons; for what son is there whom a father does not chasten? But if you are without chastening, of which all have become partakers, then you are illegitimate and not sons. Furthermore, we have had human fathers who corrected us, and we paid them respect. Shall we not much more readily be in subjection to the Father of spirits and live? (Hebrews 12:7–9 NKJV)

God doesn't prune dead branches; he prunes live branches that can generate more fruit. Jesus learned obedience through the things he suffered (Hebrew 5:11). So too must we learn obedience through the things we suffer. If God has called us into the Joseph calling, then we must seek to understand the six principle stages to discover, navigate, and fulfill our destinies.

SEEING FROM GOD'S PERSPECTIVE

When Joseph was elevated to rule over the Egyptian kingdom, he revealed some profound truths that were gained from the experiences of his years of adversity. He named his first son Manasseh "because God has made me forget all my trouble and all my father's household" (Genesis 41:51). His second son was named Ephraim because "God has made me fruitful in the land of my suffering" (v. 52).

Whenever God takes us through the land of affliction, he will do two things through that affliction: First, he will bring such healing that we will be able to forget the pain, and second, he will make us fruitful from the painful experiences. God does not waste our afflictions if we allow him the freedom to complete the work within us. His desire is to create virtue that remains during the times of testing so that he can bring us into the place of fruitfulness. He has never promised to keep us from entering the valleys of testing, but he promised to make us fruitful in them.

If you are in the valley of affliction, now is the time to press into him. When the time comes to bring you out of this valley, he will heal your memories and bring fruit from this very time. You may find yourself in the place of extreme adversity and are wondering what God is doing in your life. I often ask those who find themselves in this place if they are willing to surrender their lives completely to the purposes of God. Are you ready to surrender completely? If so, pray a prayer of surrender to God right now.

NAVIGATING THE SIX STAGES OF YOUR PURPOSE

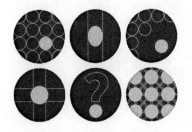

8

STAGE 1: RECRUITMENT

GOD OFTEN RECRUITS HIS SERVANTS THROUGH A CRISIS

> It may be hard for an egg to turn into a bird: it would be a jolly sight harder for it to learn to fly while remaining an egg. We are like eggs at present. And you cannot go on indefinitely being just an ordinary, decent egg. We must be hatched or go bad.
>
> —C. S. Lewis, *Mere Christianity*[1]

Recruitment through crisis is the first of the six stages of a Joseph calling. When we understand crises and how God uses them in our lives, we're less prone to make ourselves victims. Instead, we appreciate how these crises are used to make us more fulfilled and to bring us into our larger story.

The Joseph calling process can be seen in the lives of many characters in the Bible and many modern-day change agents. Leaders often have a circumstance that ushers them into the larger story of their lives. Abraham had a dream and vision, Jacob had a dream, Paul was blinded by God on the road to Damascus, David was thrust into an encounter with Goliath, Martin Luther had a crisis of theology, and Martin Luther King Jr. was thrust into the Civil Rights Movement at age twenty-six. In each case, each person was thrust into a circumstance not of their choosing that led to their ultimate assignment in life, which was rooted in their unique purpose. You cannot force that timetable; it is up to God when the time is right.

There is usually some type of *kairos* moment or crisis of belief in the life of one on whom God has placed an *extraordinary* call. Every call from God is extraordinary; however, not every call is high profile. We may not affect the masses, but we are all called to a unique assignment from God.

> Every call from God is extraordinary; however, not every call is high profile.

In the following examples of God's method of recruitment, you will see various methods of crisis he used on these individuals to begin the process of bringing each person into a realization of his unique calling for each one of them. Perhaps some of these examples will help you to understand how God is working in your own life and circumstances.

A LIFE-THREATENING CRISIS

In 2005, Ashley Smith was a single woman who had just lost custody of her child due to her addiction. Her daughter, Paige, was living with Ashley's aunt while she was fighting her drug addiction in Atlanta. Her husband had been murdered by being stabbed by drug dealers, and if things didn't change, she, too, would be a victim to drugs.

One evening while unpacking in her new apartment in an Atlanta suburb at two in the morning, she went outside to her car to get her cigarettes. As she returned to her door, a stranger forced his way in with a gun to her head. Ashley readily admits that if she had not been a drug addict, she would not have been outside at that hour.

Brian Nichols was on the run after a killing spree in downtown Atlanta, Georgia. Nichols was on trial for rape when he escaped from custody and murdered the judge presiding over his trial, a court reporter, a sheriff's deputy, and later a federal agent. After a large-scale manhunt was launched in the metropolitan Atlanta area, Nichols was taken into custody twenty-six hours later.

However, during those twenty-six hours, Ashley's apartment became his hideout. He held her hostage for seven hours, from two in the morning until nine. She was his captive. It was a life-threatening seven hours, not knowing if she might become his next victim. These hours became her motivation to give up drugs for good if she were to live through this. Nichols wanted her to take the drugs she gave him, but she refused at the risk of being killed. Somehow Ashley felt God was issuing her an ultimatum: If she took drugs that night, her life was done.

She had been given a book by a friend called *The Purpose-Driven Life* by Rick Warren.[2] She had not read much of it, but it was on her kitchen table that night. Her captor told her to read it to him. So she read to him off and on throughout the night. Ashley credits being able to read the book and connect with Nichols on a personal level with saving her life. She also thinks that God orchestrated their encounter that night. Nichols released her later that morning, and she convinced him to give up to the authorities. The prosecution charged him with committing fifty-four crimes during the escape, and he was found guilty on all counts on November 7, 2008. He is now serving multiple life sentences with no possible parole.

Today Ashley's story is captured in a major motion picture called *Captive* that was released in 2015 by Paramount Pictures. David Oyelowo, Martin Luther King Jr., in *Selma* and Kate Mara, who starred in *Fantastic Four*, star as Brian and Ashley in *Captive*.

This event has led Ashley to the larger story of her life with a ministry that allows her to share the love of Christ and to encourage those who struggle with addictions. The larger story of Ashley's life began as a major life-threatening crisis that is now an international story of hope and courage. God redeemed her life from the pit and gave her a platform to encourage others.

MARTIN LUTHER

German-born Martin Luther was living out the call of God on his life, but he wasn't living the larger story. Born on November 10, 1483, Martin was a German friar, Catholic priest, professor of theology, and seminal figure of the sixteenth-century movement in Christianity known later as the Protestant Reformation.

Initially an Augustinian friar, Martin began to read the Bible for what it said, not for what his tradition wanted it to say. Luther's reading of the Scriptures was in direct conflict with some of the practices of the Catholic Church. He began to reject several of its teachings and practices, strongly disputing the claim that freedom from God's punishment for sin could be purchased with money. Not only that, but he directly opposed indulgence salesman Johann Tetzel, a Dominican friar, with his Ninety-Five Theses in 1517.

His refusal to retract all of his writings at the demand of Pope Leo X in 1520 and the Holy Roman Emperor Charles V at the Diet of Worms in 1521 resulted in his excommunication by the pope and condemnation as an outlaw by the emperor. Such can be a consequence when being drafted into the larger story of your life.

Luther taught that salvation and subsequently eternity in heaven is not earned by good deeds but is received only as a free gift of God's grace through faith in Jesus Christ as redeemer. This redemption is primarily a redemption from sin and subsequently eternity in hell. Luther's theology challenged the authority of the pope by teaching that the Bible is the only source of divinely revealed knowledge and that all baptized Christians are a holy priesthood, not just the Catholic priests.

Those who identified with Luther's teachings became known as Lutherans, even though Luther insisted on *Christian* as the only acceptable name for individuals who professed Christ. His translation of the Bible into German instead of Latin made it more accessible, which had a tremendous impact on the church and on German culture itself. This fostered the development of a standard version of the German language, added several principles to the art of translation, and influenced the writing of an English translation, the Tyndale Bible. Just sixty years earlier, God would give a man an invention that would be used by Luther to print the Bible—Johann Gutenberg. That invention was probably the greatest invention the world had ever known, based on the impact it had on the world.[3]

Martin Luther represents a perfect example of one whose larger story was a result of a crisis in his life. Personal crisis is often the front door to discovering God's larger story for us. Little did Luther realize that his long-held faith traditions would almost cost him his very life. But he would also be the greatest spiritual reformer since Christ, giving faith and freedom to millions of people through his teaching that salvation is by faith alone in Jesus Christ alone, not by works. Luther could never have imagined he would grow up one day to be the founder of the Protestant Reformation.

> Personal crisis is often the front door to discovering God's larger story for us.

This would also be true of most who have a significant call upon their lives, which has impacted many others. What we see in Martin Luther's and others' stories to follow is that those who fulfill the larger story of their lives are rarely looking to do that; rather, it happens when a crisis takes place. The crisis becomes the front door to the larger story that God is writing for that individual.

FROM ORPHAN TO BEAUTY QUEEN
TO SAVING A NATION

Imagine that God is in heaven, and he has a discussion with his angels that goes something like this: "I am going to create a woman who will be so beautiful that I will use her beauty to win beauty contests, and ultimately save a nation." That is the story of Esther.

Esther was the most unlikely woman to save a nation. She was a Jewish orphan in Persia who was adopted by her cousin Mordecai. Esther became the queen of Persia, and God used her to thwart the genocide of her people. God gave Esther favor with the king of Persia, who ultimately saved her life and the lives of the Jewish people, and made Mordecai prime minister.

Here again we see a crisis event being used to usher someone, in this case a beautiful young orphaned woman, into a significant destiny and call. At first Esther was not sure she was willing to risk her life, because according to custom, anyone who appealed to the king without being summoned could lose his life. Mordecai challenged her and proclaimed to her, "You were born for such a time as this!" (Esther 4:4, my paraphrase).

There are times when we realize that we have been born for a particular assignment. We realize that we are placed into the time and space of God's choosing that is going to be used for a significant purpose that God wants to accomplish on the earth. Mordecai challenged Esther when she showed doubt about stepping into her God-ordained assignment. He said, "If you do not do this, then God will surely raise up another" (Esther 4:4, my paraphrase). Ouch! Mordecai was a straight shooter; he told it like it was. He had a sense that God had created this situation for her to step into.

How many times do we have situations that are ripe for our involvement, but we shy away? We think we are not suited for it, or we possibly fear we might make a mistake, or we even fear failure itself. If you are a woman reading this, then know that God created you and even your appearance for a reason. The psalmist tells us how God formed us from the foundations of the world, even what we would look like:

> For You formed my inward parts;
> You covered me in my mother's womb.
> I will praise You, for I am fearfully and wonderfully made;
> Marvelous are Your works,
> And that my soul knows very well.

My frame was not hidden from You,
When I was made in secret,
And skillfully wrought in the lowest parts of the earth.
Your eyes saw my substance, being yet unformed.
And in Your book they all were written,
The days fashioned for me,
When as yet there were none of them.
(Psalm 139:13–16 NKJV)

A TWENTY-SIX-YEAR-OLD HEARS THE TRUMPET CALL

In 1955 Rosa Parks refused to obey Montgomery, Alabama, bus driver James F. Blake's order that she give up her seat in the colored section of the bus to a white passenger, after the white section was already filled. She was working as secretary of the NAACP at the time. Parks' act of defiance and the Montgomery Bus Boycott became important symbols of the modern Civil Rights Movement.

Rosa Parks became an international icon of resistance to racial segregation and would become the lightning rod to rally around their cause. She organized and collaborated with Civil Rights leaders, including Edgar Nixon, president of the local chapter of the NAACP, and Martin Luther King Jr., a new minister who was only twenty-six years of age and who gained national prominence in the Civil Rights Movement.

This event became a tipping point that ushered Martin Luther King Jr. and Rosa Parks into the larger story of their lives. Life would now involve a series of great, and in many cases, life-threatening challenges, just like Moses had to face by going to Pharaoh. However, this time it was the US government and a stronghold of racism over a nation. God was going to use these two, as well as other leaders, to break the back of this stronghold over America. But, much like Moses, they would have to endure great hardship, and it would ultimately cost King his life. When Rosa Park died in 2005, she was the first woman and second non-US government official to lie in honor at the capitol rotunda.

Martin Luther King Jr. was named after Martin Luther, which is ironic because he would also be used as a reformer in the life of a nation. He helped to organize the 1963 march on Washington, where he delivered his famous "I Have a Dream" speech. There he established his reputation as one of the greatest orators in American history.

On October 14, 1964, King received the Nobel Peace Prize for combating racial inequality through nonviolence. He was planning a national occupation of Washington, DC, when he was assassinated on April 4, 1968, in Memphis, Tennessee. King was posthumously awarded the Presidential Medal of Freedom and the Congressional Gold Medal. Martin Luther King Jr. Day was established as a holiday in numerous cities and states beginning in 1971, and as a US federal holiday in 1986. Hundreds of streets have been renamed in his honor. In addition, a county was rededicated in his honor, and a memorial statue on the National Mall was opened to the public in 2011.[4]

Oswald Chambers explains how the recruitment process takes place in the life of those whom God greatly uses: "Whether it means life or death—it makes no difference!"[5] In Philippians 1:21, Paul was determined that nothing would stop him from doing exactly what God wanted him to do.

Before we choose to follow God's will, a crisis must develop in our lives. This happens because we tend to be unresponsive to God's gentler nudges. He brings us to the place where he asks us to be our utmost for him, and so we begin to debate. He then providentially produces a crisis whereby we must decide—for or against. That moment becomes a great crossroads. If a crisis has come to you on any front, then let me encourage you to surrender your will to Jesus absolutely and irrevocably.

God's Recruitment Strategy for Leaders

When God calls his servants into service, there is often much travail. There are many examples in the Bible where God makes his presence known through circumstances that tax the individuals to their very soul. This encounter was their entry door to their larger story:

- Consider Paul, who was stricken blind on the Damascus road.
- Consider Peter, who he denied Jesus after the crucifixion and was in total despair.
- Consider Shadrach, Meshach, and Abednego, who were thrown into the fiery furnace.
- Consider Daniel, who was thrown into the lions' den.
- Consider David, who was forced to flee his former employer for many years and lived on the run as a fugitive.

It may seem strange that God uses such incredible adversity to prepare his servants for greater service, but that is often God's way. God knows that the human heart is incapable of voluntarily stepping into situations that take us beyond our comfort zones. And so he intentionally brings us into hard places to prove and to drive us deeper into the soil of his grace.

In arid regions of the world, trees cannot survive unless their roots grow deeper to where the water can be found. Once they reach the water, those trees become stronger than trees found in tropical climates. Their root systems ensure that they can withstand any storm or drought. In the same way, God brings us into extremely difficult situations to prove his power and to drive our spiritual roots deeper.

The Role of the Valley Experience in Our Recruitment

Sometimes the recruitment process leads to death. It could be a job loss, a loss of a business, a relationship loss, or even a health issue.

This can even lead to us thinking there is nothing left in our world for which to live. In the natural, it appears that everything is against us, and we may even believe God has abandoned us. But this is not the truth, as we know that God never leaves us nor forsakes us (Hebrews 13:5). During these times, God is doing his deepest behind-the-scenes work. He is performing a deeper work in each of us, a work that cannot be seen.

When clients began leaving my ad agency in the '90s for no apparent reason and it dried up, my wife left me, and I lost my wealth through a "Bernie Madoff" type of scam, it appeared that everything was against me. I could not see that God was orchestrating a whole new calling on my life. At the time, it seemed like the worst thing in the world was happening. It seemed as if I had been a failure. But all the years before had been preparation for what God's ultimate calling would be on my life.

One of God's methods for directing his children's steps is through drying up resources, a job loss, a career change, or some other kind of disaster. In these times, we are willing to listen more intently and to seek God in ways we would not normally do. C. S. Lewis once wrote, "God whispers to us in our pleasures, speaks in our conscience, but shouts in our pains; it is His megaphone to rouse a deaf world."[6]

God turned my valley of trouble into a door of hope for hundreds of thousands of people around the world by leading me to begin writing about my experiences. This led to writing TGIF, which is read by hundreds of thousands of people each day in over a hundred nations. It has also taken me to twenty-six nations to teach and equip men and women in the body of Christ. God turned my mess into messages and made me a messenger.

There is a time in the life of every leader when the trumpet sounds. It is up to us to step into the larger story by sensing the moment and allowing God to move us into that story. It will never be comfortable or convenient at the time. Let me encourage you to consider your life circumstance as a possible trumpet blast that might bring you into the larger story of your life. Friend, God may take you through times when you will question his love. In such times, you must cling to his coattails so that you see his purposes in it. Do not throw away your confidence; it will be richly rewarded.

> You need to persevere so that when you have done the will of God, you will receive what he has promised. For,
> "In just a very little while,
> he who is coming will come
> and will not delay."

And,

> "But My righteous one will live by faith.
> And I take no pleasure
> in the one who shrinks back." (Hebrews 10:36–38)

Though it is not often popular today to say so, God often recruits his servants through a crisis. Are you going through a crisis? It may be that God has just begun the process of the Joseph calling in your life.

STAGE 2: CHARACTER DEVELOPMENT

GOD DEVELOPS HIS SERVANTS THROUGH A SERIES OF CHARACTER TESTS

We go from glory to glory, but it's hell in the hallway.

— Bishop Joseph Garlington[1]

Sometimes God will place you in situations in which you have no natural gifting. In these cases, it is important to understand that God puts you there to experience his power so you can accomplish your tasks. This is a season of character building.

Joseph went through a thirteen-year season of character building and preparation. It was hardly an "assignment" that matched his purpose. His primary assignment to fulfill God's call included this painful process. God takes many leaders through a season of character building that often has little to do with their natural gifts, but it is a vital step toward developing the character that God requires for the assignment he has for that person.

I first met Tom Stansbury in 1997 in Mississippi at an International Christian Chamber of Commerce meeting. I was in the middle of my seven-year pit experience. Tom and I developed a friendship and later participated in some international marketplace conferences together. Tom was just beginning to walk in an understanding of integrating faith into his work life.

Tom's spiritual heritage goes back to the early days of the Jesus Movement when he lived in a Christian commune in Northern California at a place called the Lighthouse Ranch, a ministry of Gospel Outreach, back in the early 1980s.

Tom's growing up years were difficult. His father was an entrepreneur in the oil business who died when Tom was just three years old. His mother was divorced and remarried five times. Tom married in 1987 and had two children from that marriage, but left his wife in 2001 to have an affair with another woman. Tom's wife Paula divorced him in 2003, and he married the other woman and had a son from that marriage. After seven years of this marriage, it would also end in divorce, and Tom's life was in a crisis.

I reached out to Tom during those years, only to be rejected. He was in an all-out rebellion toward God and his own family. I eventually lost contact with Tom. One thing I have learned over the years about sin is this: You cannot take territory from the devil if he still has territory in you. Yielding to sin will always overcome you.

> You cannot take territory from the devil if he still has territory in you.

God eventually began to draw Tom back into relationship with himself. He came to understand he was living as a businessman poser, hiding behind a façade of position and power, living to the perceptions and expectations of others as he became more and more successful. Tom had to get to the bottom before he could begin to look up; he had to recognize the core issues that drove him to make his poor decisions.

Seeking to find his identity in a woman only led to promiscuity and addictions. We cannot use any area of the flesh to bring about a spiritual end. Men, beware of taking the question of your manhood to a woman. This must come from our heavenly Father alone. When you have unresolved pain in your life, a woman can often be the perceived solution to your pain, but she will never satisfy.

The Bible tells us that satan wants to steal, kill, and destroy our lives (John 10:10). The enemy set the table for what took place in Tom's life. C. S. Lewis once said, "The long, dull, monotonous years of middle-aged prosperity or middle-aged adversity are excellent campaigning weather for the devil."[2] When I looked at Tom, I saw two biblical personalities—David and Peter.

David was a passionate man who made wrong choices in his early life. His sin with Bathsheba and the death of his son were the two major life events that brought David to the bottom. But God responded to David's repentance and allowed the Savior of the world to come from the family line of Bathsheba. I find that truly amazing.

Likewise, Peter was an impulsive man. He responded quickly to situations without thinking of the consequences. He often responded to Jesus only to have to repent for not following through on his commitments. Jesus even rebuked satan in Peter when Peter argued with the Lord about Jesus' future death. He told Jesus he would never betray him, but then went on to betray him three times in the twenty-four-hour period just before Jesus' crucifixion.

Shattered dreams often become the unexpected doorways to a destiny we could never appreciate without them. God has an amazing ability to turn our sin into something that will be used to build his kingdom when we turn completely away from our sin. Today Tom is a different person. He has reconciled with both of his wives and his children. He is single and living victoriously in his singleness.

Today, Tom is moving in God's presence beyond his own natural gifting, rising from the valley of dry bones (see Ezekiel 37). *Through his own transformation as a leader, he is now on a mission to serve other leaders through his leadership development company, transformedleader.com.* He believes he has an assignment from God to "mobilize ten thousand marketplace leaders to transform a hundred nations." We are seeing signs and wonders occur in Tom's life, and the verse "Where sin abounded, grace abounded much more" (Romans 5:20 NKJV) holding true!

Larry Crabb once said, "I've come to believe that only broken people truly worship."[3] When you truly come to realize what you have been forgiven of, then you will never return to the life you had before. God never leads people into sin to create a testimony, but he will turn all things into good when we give our lives completely to him and allow him to deal with our past (Romans 8:28).

JESUS WAS TESTED—SO ARE WE

A test always follows a victory. Such was the case for Jesus. The Bible says that the Spirit of God drove Jesus into the wilderness right after his baptism and the Father's audible proclamation of Jesus as the Son of God (Mark 1:11). Jesus was led to the desert by the Spirit to be tempted by satan during his forty days of fasting in the wilderness. He was tempted in three core areas, and we are tested in the same areas:

1. *Identity.* Satan said, "If you are the Son of God," then do this (Matthew 4:3, 6). The devil wants us to find our identity in other places, not in God. He wants us to find our identity in our work, our money, or in our status. But our identity must be in Christ alone.

2. *Authority.* Satan tempts us to use our own power to do whatever we want instead of placing our dependence on God. He wants us to live through our flesh. God says we are to trust in the Lord with all our hearts.

3. *Source of provision.* "If you are God, then feed yourself. Do not depend on God" (Matthew 4:3, my paraphrase). Satan wants us to believe our provision is not from God, but through our sweat and toil. But we need to know that God is the source of all our provision.

As human beings, we are faced with these same three temptations daily. God has given Tom a vision to raise up Christians in the marketplace to be change agents in the culture. He desires to raise up the dry bones of leaders who are not living for Christ.

In the book of Ezekiel, we find a prophetic verse that speaks of dry bones that have no life in them. These represent the millions of lives who do not have the life of Jesus in them. But God wants to bring life to every one of them.

> Then [God] said to me, "Prophesy to these bones and say to them, 'Dry bones, hear the word of the LORD! This is what the Sovereign LORD says to these bones: I will make breath enter you, and you will come to life. I will attach tendons to you and make flesh come upon you and cover you with skin; I will put breath in you, and you will come to life. Then you will know that I am the LORD.'"
>
> So I prophesied as I was commanded. And as I was prophesying, there was a noise, a rattling sound, and the bones came together, bone to bone. I looked, and tendons and flesh appeared on them and skin covered them, but there was no breath in them. (Ezekiel 37:4–8)

God is calling forth his sons and daughters to step into their destinies: "For the creation waits in eager expectation for the children of God to be revealed" (Romans 8:19). The temple was made up of the outer court, the inner court, and the Holy of Holies, where only the priest could go on behalf of the people, and at that only once a year. A walk with God is about living in the inner court with God versus the outer court of performance and posturing.

RECONCILING FAILURE

Some might say that with all the moral failures of Tom, how could I ever trust him? That is a fair question. There is a principle that surrounds failure: Failure is often the stepping-stone to greater victory. Henry Ford once said, "Failure is simply the opportunity to begin again, this time more intelligently."[4] This is especially true in our walk with God. We should never let the pain of the past steal God's vision for our future.

Sometimes people live in their past; they allow their past to dictate their future. We often allow satan to constantly remind us of our past failures and mistakes. When this happens, we must go to the cross and remind satan that we are covered by the blood of Jesus that was shed on the cross. When God looks at our sin, he no longer sees it. Rather, he sees the blood of Christ covering our sin. The psalmist confirmed this when he declared, "As far as the east is from the west, so far has he removed our transgressions from us" (Psalm 103:12).

A close mutual friend of Tom and mine, Ford Taylor, often says, "Change seldom occurs until the pain of staying the same exceeds the pain of change!" Sometimes the Lord leaves us in a problem until we have had enough pain to get rid of it forever. Sometimes we must get to a deep level of pain and disappointment in life in order to be motivated for real change. The pain to remain the same must exceed the pain to change. We don't want to only change a habit; we want a real transformational change of our natures.

> Sometimes we must get to a deep level of pain and disappointment in life in order to be motivated for real change.

Graham Cooke explains how sin affects our lives:

When we resist God, contraction occurs; we get smaller in the spirit. But when we submit to the Spirit, an expansion happens. Our heart is enlarged as we submit to God's hand. Our faith increases. We grow so rapidly that we push the enemy's territory into itself. The space in which he works contracts. Suddenly, the enemy has no room to operate.[5]

Sometimes God frustrates our desire to experience him to deepen our experience in him. God's process often involves failing miserably at something, learning the lesson or lessons of the failure, walking in the new truth successfully, and then teaching it to others.

Failure is often God's greatest tool for success in the kingdom. Jesus didn't choose the most qualified, the most successful, or those who had it all together; rather, he chose those who made themselves available to him. He didn't choose ability; he chose availability. Our failures become our authority once we learn the lessons of the failure. Peter's denial of Jesus ultimately led to him being the leader of the early church.

JESUS' VIEW OF FAILURE

I am often amazed at how Jesus dealt with failure in his disciples. When he revealed himself to them after the resurrection, he did not shame them or communicate his disappointment with them. When he saw them for the first time, he said, "Peace be with you!" (John 20: 19). He did not say, "Hey, you guys all betrayed me. What's up with that?"

When the angel of the Lord came to Gideon in the wheat press, he called him "mighty warrior" (Judges 6:12). Gideon at that time was a fearful, angry-at-God farmer simply trying to avoid being killed by his enemies. God always looks at what we are becoming, not at what we are. He does not look at our past or our current condition, but he sees his plans for us. How comforting this is to know about the nature of God. Satan always defines our lives based on our past; God defines us by our future.

The darkest times take place just before the daylight breaks through. Never let the fear of failure keep you from the prospects for success. Failing forward makes us one step closer to success. God doesn't test us to find out something he already knows; he tests us to let us know ourselves so we can grow into maturity. If you hope to succeed, then learn everything you can from your failures. God sees failure as preparation for success. Some things are only discovered by the desperate soul.

Sara Blakely is the founder of Spanx, a women's garment company with sales of more than four hundred million annually. She said her father taught her the greatest lesson in life: "He used to encourage me to fail. He told me to try things and never let failure discourage me from continuing to try. This one thing has kept me from fearing failure. He told me to see failure as a stepping-stone to success."[6]

This should also serve as a rebuke to all who condemn those who have failed. We must be careful not to judge others. "Whatever judgment you use for others will be used to judge you," Jesus said (Matthew 7:2, my paraphrase). People often keep us in the role of our past. We must be given freedom to change. When trusting those who have had failure in their pasts, it is appropriate to take baby steps to trust them but also verify progress. We must have certain boundaries when we extend our trust to provide opportunities for that person to grow and receive greater trust. Also, if we allow others to define us based on our past, then we have made that person an idol. We have let them define us instead of allowing God to define us. God is the only hero we can have.

We Are Called to Transformation

God uses the character-development phase to transform us by the power of Christ. He is preparing us to be usable in his kingdom. Read how Paul describes this transformational process in *The Message* translation of the Bible:

> Don't become so well-adjusted to your culture that you fit into it without even thinking. Instead, fix your attention on God. You'll be changed from the inside out. Readily recognize what he wants from you, and quickly respond to it. Unlike the culture around you, always dragging you down to its level of immaturity, God brings the best out of you, develops well-formed maturity in you. (Romans 12:2 MSG)

The gospel is free, but maturity is not; it will cost something. God gives us visions on the mountain but leads us into the valley to work out those visions. In order to bring heaven to earth, we are often required to go through hell on earth—much like Paul did. Madame Guyon once said, "I have learned to love the darkness of sorrow, for it is there I see the brightness of God's face."[7] The lives of Moses, Joseph, and Gideon tell us that God puts weakness together with his strength. The valley experience is often the training ground.

God often allows us to go low in order to go high with God. The more favor you get from God, the more intentionally you must go lower. There is no growth to maturity without this process. I have a friend who often says, "Beware of any Christian leader who does not walk with a limp." We must submit to this process of sanctification if the enemy is to submit to us. The maturity process is the foundation for developing our obedience, which results in our authority. Jesus learned obedience from the things he suffered. There is no authority without this submission to the process of learning obedience. In fact, God gives us greater authority as we increase in victory over our past sin. Then he uses it to pay back the enemy for trying to destroy us.

David, after his sin with Bathsheba, realized that he was not living a life of purity and integrity, and so he penned these words: "Behold, You desire truth in the inward parts, and in the hidden part You will make me to know wisdom" (Psalm 51:6 NKJV). And Gordon Dalbey said, "A man becomes spiritually mature when he is more afraid that the truth will *not* be told than that it will be told."[8]

> Overcoming a crisis always leads to elevation and greater spiritual authority.

Do not allow yourself to be elevated beyond where your integrity can keep you. If you don't have integrity now, then you won't have it when God elevates you. You never know your level of purity until it is tested. David failed the purity test. You can't be truthful with crowds if you are not truthful alone. Heinz Ketchup founder, H. J. Heinz, once said, "Quality is for a product what character is to a man."[9]

HUMILITY: GOD'S MOST IMPORTANT CHARACTER REQUIREMENT

God requires humility in his leaders, which can come either voluntarily or involuntarily. Getting it voluntarily is much preferred. There is a principle I have observed: Overcoming a crisis always leads to elevation and greater spiritual authority. And humility is the key attribute God values in his leaders.

Humility leads to unity with Jesus and the Father; that unity leads to spiritual authority; and that spiritual authority leads to influence in the lives of others. One writer put it this way:

> The person whose faith has been severely tested, yet who has come through the battle victoriously, is the person to whom even greater tests will come. The finest jewels are those that are the most carefully cut and polished, and the most precious metals are put through the hottest fires. You can be sure Abraham would never have been called the Father of Faith had he not been tested to the utmost.[10]

ADVERSITY IS NOT ALWAYS ROOTED IN SIN

Joseph is our classic story of God using adversity to prepare a leader for his assignment. Joseph did not commit sin that caused his thirteen years of hardship, although he certainly was not tactful in sharing his dream with his brothers who were already jealous of his father's favoritism toward him. But God used those thirteen years of preparation to remove pride from his life and to test him at every level. It prepared him for his eighty-one-year assignment. Visions make leaders passionate; thorns keep them authentic.

BROKENNESS BECOMES YOUR STRENGTH

There is an oxymoron throughout the Bible: brokenness is strength (1 Samuel 2:4). How can this be? How can brokenness be strength? In order to use men and women to their fullest extent, the Lord has to break his servants so that they might have a new kind of strength that is not human in origin. It is strength in spirit, which is born only through brokenness. Paul was broken on the Damascus road; Peter was broken after Jesus was taken prisoner; Jacob was broken at Peniel; David was broken after his sin with Bathsheba. The list could go on of those the Lord had to break in different ways before they could be used in the kingdom.

When we are broken, we see the frailty of human strength and come to grips with the reality that we can do nothing in our own strength. It is only then that new strength emerges. God resists the proud, but he gives grace to the humble. Do not fear brokenness, for it may be the missing ingredient to a life that emerges with a new kind of strength and experience not known before.

ARE YOU READY TO PRAY THE MOST DANGEROUS PRAYER ON EARTH?

The most important thing in your life is yielding your life fully to Jesus Christ and his purposes. Are you willing to pray the most dangerous prayer? If you are willing, here is an outline prayer to follow:

Lord, I fully surrender my life to you today. I invite you to be Lord of my life—my circumstances and my past. I renounce all sin, and I give you permission to do anything if it will fulfill your complete purpose and destiny for me. Amen.

The real danger now is only for satan and his kingdom as you become God's instrument to bring heaven on earth as his representative. Are you ready for that assignment?

STAGE 3: ISOLATION

GOD ISOLATES HIS LEADERS
TO TURN MESSES INTO MESSAGES

Without reflection, we go blindly on our way, creating more
unintended consequences, and failing to achieve anything
useful.

—Margaret J. Wheatley, *Finding Our Way*[1]

S tage three of our six stages to discovering, navigating, and fulfilling your destiny is the isolation stage. It is a time when we
become isolated and often experience deep feelings of loneliness
and abandonment. If we are not careful at this stage, this time can
be dangerous to our psyche, and we can fall prey to many kinds of
sin in an effort to cope. However, it can be a fruitful season if we
allow God to enter that time with us.

The apostle Paul tells us in Galatians of some of the facts surrounding his own conversion. He clearly understood the call Jesus
placed on his life—he did not have to consult with others about
this calling. But before he was released to begin his own mission,
he went to Arabia for three years and stayed in the desert. Why did
Paul have to go to Arabia for three years before he ever met another
disciple of Jesus Christ?

The Bible does not tell us plainly why Paul spent three years in
Arabia. However, based upon many examples of God placing special calls on individuals' lives, we know it often requires a time of

separation between the old life and the new one. No doubt, Paul had plenty of time to consider what had taken place in his heart, and so he had time to develop an intimate knowledge and relationship with his newfound Savior. His life was about to change dramatically.

So often, when God places a call on one of his children, it requires a separation from the old life. There is a time of being away from the old in order to prepare the heart for what is about to come. It can be a painful and difficult separation indeed. Joseph was separated from his family; Jacob was sent to live with his uncle Laban; Moses was sent to the desert.

When God began a deeper work in my own life, it required a separation from all I had known before. He removed all that I had placed confidence in up to that point. It was painful and scary since I was in my mid forties. In my mind, it was not the time to start life over. I had been making plans for early retirement, but God had a different idea. He removed all my comforts and securities to accomplish a much greater work than what I could see at the time. Even though it was scary, the picture is clear now. I understand why it was necessary, even though I didn't at the time.

David must have been thinking these thoughts as he looked out over the rocky cliffs below from his cave. Rejected. A fugitive. A man without a country. No army. No resources. He had just faked madness so he could stay alive. He must have had a sick stomach. Proverbs 13:12 tells us, "Hope deferred makes the heart sick." How did life get to this dead end? Such can be the fate of a leader in whom God is doing a deeper work. David must have identified with the same feelings as Job when he too could not make sense of his calamities. Job lamented:

> But if I go to the east, he is not there;
>> if I go to the west, I do not find him.
> When he is at work in the north, I do not see him;
>> when he turns to the south, I catch no glimpse of him.

> But he knows the way that I take;
>> when he has tested me, I will come forth as gold.
> My feet have closely followed his steps;
>> I have kept to his way without turning aside.
> I have not departed from the commands of his lips;
>> I have treasured the words of his mouth more than
>>> my daily bread.
> (Job 23:8–12)

God handpicked David to be the heir to King Saul's throne over Israel. He removed Saul due to his disobedience; he instructed the prophet Samuel to make a house call to Jesse's family. Jesse had eight sons, and one of them was to be the next king of Israel. In one day, God took David from delivering lunch to delivering a nation.

David was a man whose character was tested, much like Joseph. After David was anointed by Samuel to be the next king, he did not immediately go to *king-to-be* training school. The Bible tells us he went back to shepherding his father's sheep. When we get a dramatic word from God, how many of us want to go out and try to fulfill that word immediately, rather than wait for God to fulfill it in his timing?

Soon after this commissioning by Samuel, God orchestrated the events that would bring David into the first phase of his calling to be the king of the nation of Israel. Although merely a teenager, he was invited to serve Saul through his musical abilities. This is noteworthy. We see something of David's personal devotional life with God. He was a musician and worshiper before he was a warrior. We all must be worshipers of God in our personal lives. David became a source of comfort for Saul when he played for him. The truth is that you never know when God is going to choose to elevate you to a place of influence.

Once the access door was opened, God orchestrated another opportunity for David. David volunteered to fight Goliath when no other soldier, including Saul himself, would fight him. He also inquired as to what the benefit would be if someone defeated Goliath. The man who defeated Goliath would not have to pay taxes, would receive a financial reward, and get the king's daughter in marriage. David concluded that the reward was worth the risk. He was given a platform to demonstrate God's favor on his skills as a warrior, even at a young age. He also understood covenant with God, and he spoke with authority: "Who is this uncircumcised Philistine that he should defy the armies of the living God?" (1 Samuel 17:26).

David killed Goliath and solved a big problem for Saul and all of Israel. The greatest miracle in this story is not his defeat of Goliath, but that King Saul risked the entire Israeli army on the merits of a teenager. This should have been Saul's battle to fight. However, David defeated Goliath and won the hearts of all Israel in the process. And it was this favor from God that increased as David won more battles.

This victory also caused jealousy and insecurity to grow in Saul, which led to Saul's later decision to try to kill David. David had to flee as a fugitive for doing his job well. Sometimes obedience does not yield less adversity; it actually increases it. Have you ever done your job so well that others become jealous of you? David became a fugitive for being great at what God called him to do. Many successful people have become ostracized by the jealousy of others. They become the target.

> The training ground for a leader in the kingdom of God can often mean years of difficult, unfair treatment.

The training ground for a leader in the kingdom of God can often mean years of difficult, unfair treatment. David was forced to flee from Saul, and he was tested to see if he would take things into his own hands. Although Saul was wrong in what he was doing, David understood it was not his right to remove Saul from power. He recognized the importance of the office rather than the weakness of the individual in the office; David knew it was God who placed people in their places of power. It is quite amazing that he understood this principle given his age. David passed this test with flying colors in spite of his followers advising him to kill Saul and affirming to him that he would be justified in doing so.

DAVID'S LOW POINT

David's low point came when he had to escape the fury of Saul by running to the cave of Adullam. Alone in his cave, David may have felt abandoned by God. I'm sure he asked the question, "Is this how you train the next king of Israel?" But such are the ways of God. In fact, the ways of God are often fraught with what we perceive as unfairness, crisis, isolation, and doubts on the road to leadership.

David wrote three psalms while he was in this cave. The first psalm is Psalm 142, which gives us the condition of his heart. It is the absolute low point of his life. Listen to what he writes:

> I cry aloud to the LORD;
>> I lift up my voice to the LORD for mercy.
> I pour out before him my complaint;
>> before him I tell my trouble.
> When my spirit grows faint within me,
>> it is you who watch over my way.
> In the path where I walk
>> people have hidden a snare for me.
> Look and see, there is no one at my right hand;
>> no one is concerned for me.
> I have no refuge;
>> no one cares for my life.
> I cry to you, LORD;
>> I say, "You are my refuge,
>> my portion in the land of the living."
> Listen to my cry
>> for I am in desperate need;

rescue me from those who pursue me,
  for they are too strong for me.
Set me free from my prison,
  that I may praise your name.
Then the righteous will gather about me
  because of your goodness to me.
LORD, hear my prayer,
  listen to my cry for mercy;
in your faithfulness and righteousness
  come to my relief.
(Psalm 142:1–143:1)

David was a man looking for purpose in all of his struggles. He probably wondered how he got from being a king's favored son to being an outlaw and having to fake madness just to stay alive. He probably thought often of the day when Samuel anointed him as the next king of Israel as a teen.

Like many of us, he thought, *So where are you now, God? I thought I was your man.* It is clear David had these thoughts, but he also exhibits amazing faith and hope in God at the conclusion of this psalm: "Then the righteous will gather about me because of your goodness to me" (Psalm 142:7). It takes courage to make such a statement in the face of total defeat. He wrote in another psalm: "Whoever dwells in the shelter of the Most High will rest in the shadow of the Almighty. I will say of the LORD, 'He is my refuge and my fortress, my God, in whom I trust'" (Psalm 91:1–2).

God is working while his servants wait. Each person is being selected for a handpicked assignment. This waiting on God is preparation for a greater depth of use and a greater anointing that cannot be accomplished otherwise. In fact, the waiting period only adds to the authority that is given, creating a level of authority for you to carry out your assignment from God.

My friend and intercessor Bradley Stuart once said to me, "God doesn't prune dead trees, only fruitful ones." Nevertheless, the process can be extremely painful. I have written my best works during times of isolation and adversity, which forced me into the soil of God's grace as a result of desperation and pain.

COME OUT OF THE STRONGHOLD

God doesn't allow us to remain in our cave of isolation for too long. If we remain there too long, we become defeated by our circumstances. It is interesting what the prophet told David to do: "But the prophet Gad said to David, 'Do not stay in the stronghold. Go into the land of Judah'" (1 Samuel 22:5). *Judah* means praise. If we are to overcome our circumstances, then we must do something that seems unnatural—we need to praise God in the midst of our circumstances. It is important to make the distinction that we don't praise him *for* the circumstance, but we praise him for *who he is* in the midst of them—he is our deliverer. Isaiah wrote that the anointing of God's Spirit comes upon us:

> To console those who mourn in Zion,
> To give them beauty for ashes,
> The oil of joy for mourning,
> The garment of praise for the spirit of heaviness;
> That they may be called trees of righteousness,
> The planting of the LORD, that He may be glorified.
> (Isaiah 61:3 NKJV)

If handled correctly, others will be drawn to your anointing, and they will find themselves transformed as you allow your anointing to destroy the yoke of bondage in their lives. It will fall off you, and your anointing will fall onto others you serve.

We must be careful not to usurp the position of any other *anointed ones* in our midst (our Sauls), nor try to hasten our coming out of the cave. God's timing is perfected in our *waiting*. This is where he prepares us to lead those he will entrust under our care to become the mighty army of the living God. We must stand and watch what the Lord does for those who wait upon him. We must invest our lives into the nameless men and women in the workplace whom God calls us to serve.

What did the cave do in the life of David? Well, God used the mess of the cave to turn David into one of our greatest messengers, who wrote much of the Psalms, which have comforted millions of people over the centuries. We learn the lessons from tears he shed in these times, and they are a spring from which we deeply drink: "As they pass through the Valley of Baka [weeping], they make it a place of springs; the autumn rains also cover it with pools. They go from strength to strength, till each appears before God in Zion" (Psalm 84:6–7). We realize that it is only the Lord who can illumine our path during these dark times: "You, LORD, are my lamp; the LORD turns my darkness into light" (2 Samuel 22:29).

God will use your greatest failure or greatest sorrow to be a powerful force in your life and in the lives of others. We will all enter the cave of Adullam at some time in our lives if we are called to bring influence in the kingdom of God. Doubt may be such a cave. Persecution may be such a cave. Sickness may be such a cave. Bereavement may be such a cave. Conflict and betrayal in relationships can be found in this cave as well. However, there is no cave dark enough to shut out God, although it may certainly feel like it. The Bible says God will never leave us or forsake us, but he never said it would not feel like he has at times. This is the dark night of the soul. Adullam was a place of safety for David, but it was more than that—it was a place to do business with God. Your isolation stage is also that place.

If God calls us into darkness in order to enter his presence, then that darkness will become an entry to new levels of relationship with a God who longs for fellowship with us. God was testing David's mettle and preparing him for a new chapter in his life.

Charles Swindoll describes the role that isolation and the cave may play in a believer's journey:

> David has been brought to the place where God can truly begin to shape him and use him. When the sovereign God brings us to nothing, it is to reroute our life, not to end it. Human perspective says, "Aha, you've lost this, you've lost that. You've caused this, you've caused that. You've ruined this, you've ruined that. End your life!" But God says, "No. No. You're in the cave. But that doesn't mean it's curtains. That means it's time to reroute your life. Now's the time to start anew!" That's exactly what He does with David.[2]

What happens next is truly remarkable. David's family and the down-and-outers of society all come to his hideout. Now let me ask you: Which is worse, being in a cave all alone or being in a cave with your family and four hundred dysfunctional misfits in society? David has a following. This is a sign of true leadership. Are others willing to follow you?

This group of guys join him in the fight. They become his army of misfits. And after he trains them for battle, they become known as David's mighty men. David never lost a battle with these men. Such are the ways of God. He takes broken things and transforms them into weapons for kingdom warfare. David was first used to solve a problem for Israel, to replace Saul's ungodly leadership with godly leadership. But David began a new phase of training his men as a network, or in this case, his army.

Isolation May Come Because of Our Sin

Some of us may not enter our cave of isolation as a result of the call of God upon our lives; rather, we may enter because of our pride, arrogance, and presumption. However, God uses even this cave of isolation to deliver us from generational iniquity, which causes us to be un-Christlike and leads us to make decisions that send us into this cave. God will use this time to sanctify our lives for the purpose and calling he has for us, if we are willing to repent and gain the freedom this process is designed to achieve. At other times, this can come as the result of the call on our lives.

Those God uses to significantly impact his kingdom are often required to experience the deepest levels of adversity, which will light the torch to illuminate the often-dark passageways for those yet to follow. They are our teachers. And the teacher must always know the lesson better than the student. God's desire is to bring us into maturity and joy, and to help us to discover our true selves and purpose in him.

TIME IN THE DESERT REMOVES
THINGS THAT HINDER US

God knows the stubborn human heart. He knows that if he is to accomplish his deepest work within us, then he must take us into isolation so he can give us the privilege of being used in his kingdom. Isolation changes us and removes what hinders us. God uses isolation to force us to draw deep upon his grace. Isolation is only for a season—when God has accomplished what he wants through the isolation, then he will bring us out.

For some, God gives us a mission that can only be fulfilled after we have spent adequate time in preparation in the desert, which is another form of isolation. The prophet tells us in Hosea 2:14–15: "Therefore, I am now going to allure her; I will lead her into the wilderness and speak tenderly to her. There I will give her back her vineyards, and will make the Valley of Achor a door of hope." Coming out of Egypt required passing through the desert. The Hebrew word for *desert* is *midbaar*, which comes from the word *dahbaar*, meaning "to speak." Fear not the desert, for it is here where you will hear God's voice. The desert may mean being put on the shelf for a season, but from your perch you will experience the reality of a living God like never before.

It's Often Dark Before There Is Light

Abraham went through a time of isolation. God did not speak to him for thirteen long years. Whenever God gives you a vision and darkness follows, that is the time to wait. God will bring the vision to reality if you will wait on his timing. Those years of darkness played a role in the life of Abraham. It was during those years that all his self-sufficiency was destroyed. He moved away from depending on his own common sense. Silence from God was used as a time of discipline, not a period of God's displeasure.

During these times, we need to ask ourselves if we trust God or the flesh. God allows times like these so that we will know God is real. As soon as he becomes real to us, people and other sources of trust fade away. Nothing that others do or say can ever take us off the path God has for us.

> Whenever God gives you a vision and darkness follows, that is the time to wait.

When David left his cave of isolation, he said of God: "He brought me out into a spacious place; he rescued me because he delighted in me" (2 Samuel 22:20). Jesus chose times of isolation with his disciples to explain parables to them. The times when we are alone and away from the distractions of life can be the most productive times for us to hear the voice of God. But we need to initiate these times ourselves by meeting with God in the early morning.

There are other times when God initiates these times in order to get our undivided attention for the work he may be preparing for us to do. This may come in the form of an unpleasant circumstance, like a job loss, illness, or marriage separation. C. S. Lewis once wrote, "God whispers to us in our pleasures, speaks in our conscience, but shouts in our pains: it is his megaphone to rouse a deaf world."[3]

GOD TURNS MESSES INTO MESSAGES

The cave is also a place to process our pain and receive a message from God for our own lives and for the benefit of others. Many a servant of God has been placed in her own cave, which has resulted in divine revelations that have benefited the body of Christ. Daniel coined these words about the cave experience: "He reveals deep and hidden things; he knows what lies in the darkness, and light dwells with him" (Daniel 2:22). Job tells us that "he reveals the deep things of darkness and brings utter darkness into the light" (Job 12:22). And Isaiah tells us that God will reveal secret things in hidden places from our time of hiddenness: "I will give you hidden treasure, riches stored in secret places, so that you may know that I am the LORD, the God of Israel, who summons you by name" (Isaiah 45:3).

Pilgrim's Progress was written by John Bunyan because of twelve years of hiddenness in a jail cell. Nelson Mandela was hidden for twenty-seven years before he became the "Joseph" of his nation. The apostle Paul wrote many letters from his prison cell. And John the apostle wrote his vision of Revelation in total isolation on the Island of Patmos.

FROM ABUSE TO PRISON TO PRAISE

Pamela is a woman God delivered from a thirty-five-year addiction to cocaine by sending her to prison for eighteen months. Sexually abused as a child, the pain of that abuse, which continued into her teen years, was so traumatic that it led her into a life of cocaine addiction and sin to cope with the pain. She came to Christ in her late twenties. It took an eighteen-month prison term to give Pamela the solitude she needed to deal with her issues. It was during this time that she threw herself upon the mercy of God and began to memorize Scripture and recite it aloud daily. That became the breakthrough for her. No self-help program or addiction program helped her. It was God who helped Pamela overcome the issues through the fire of the Holy Spirit and the memorization of Scriptures while she was in her place of isolation and solitude.

She said, "My *vacation* was the best thing that could have happened to me. Isolation and imprisonment actually became the ticket to my freedom. God truly turned my mess into a message and made me a messenger for others who have had similar experiences to mine." Today Pamela has a ministry to women in prison called LifeChangers Legacy. Her ministry helps women who struggle with their own life circumstances that try to steal, kill, and destroy their lives (chebarministries.org).

In August of 2015, I met Pamela for the first time in Atlanta at a movie preview for *Captive*. We had both been single for many years, and I invited her to lunch to learn more about her story because she told me a movie had been planned about her life. It wasn't long before we realized God was doing something between us. We were married on May 7, 2016, and her story is being told in a new book and future movie. We often say God is a "suddenly God" who redeems our lives and gives us new beginnings. I often say, "I got captivated at *Captive*."

You never know the role solitude and isolation will play in the life of a person. For Pamela, it played the role of deliverance through the forgiveness of all those who had wronged her and the forgiveness toward herself … from the inside out. This is often the way of God.

The prophet Jeremiah understood isolation. While Jeremiah was still confined in the courtyard of the guards, the word of the Lord came to him a second time, saying: "Call to me and I will answer you and tell you great and unsearchable things you do not know" (Jeremiah 33:3). Notice that while Jeremiah was confined, the word of the Lord came to him. Sometimes God intentionally hides his people for a season to accomplish a deeper work of crafting a message through that life. "In the shelter of your presence you hide them" (Psalm 31:20).

ISOLATION CAN BE A TEMPTATION

Isolation can be a place of temptation for many. Some people have never had to be alone before. This is especially difficult for extroverts. They need people around them.

I have a friend who was a new believer. He had a sinful lifestyle before coming to Christ. He was an outgoing and engaging personality. He lived with me for a short time, as he was in a major transition in his life. He was growing in Christ and having an impact on others. He stopped drinking and was in regular fellowship with other believers. Then he moved into an apartment by himself.

His job kept him from attending church or fellowshiping with other believers. Gradually he began to drink again, and I noticed he was not calling me to grab a meal together. He later confided that he had backslidden and simply found it too difficult to be alone, and his lack of Christian fellowship contributed to opening himself up to sin once again. Living alone can be difficult at times. One must be intentional about seeking out fellowship with believers, because we cannot be an island unto ourselves. We are not made to live our Christian lives alone. We need one another in the body of Christ.

Today, temptation for men is constantly at our doorstep. One click and you can satisfy your loneliness through what you perceive can medicate your pain. But that will never satisfy. The psalmist tells us:

> Then they believed his promises
>> and sang his praise.
> But they soon forgot what he had done
>> and did not wait for his plan to unfold.
> In the desert they gave in to their craving;
>> in the wilderness they put God to the test.

So he gave them what they asked for,
    but sent a wasting disease among them.
(Psalm 106:12–15)

Once we have tasted the goodness of the Lord, we can never go back to our sinful lifestyle and find meaning and purpose. Friend, if you find yourself in a time of isolation, then allow God to use that time to build intimacy with him and seek out other believers in whom you can find fellowship.

THE WAITING PERIOD

There have been many saints in whom God used the isolation chamber to deposit something significant that was later used to minister to those who would follow behind. In all cases, there was a waiting period that had to be endured. Abraham had to wait for Isaac until it was God's timing, not his. Moses waited forty years before God spoke to him at the burning bush. Elijah waited beside the brook until he was physically and emotionally strong enough to continue his mission. Paul was hidden away for three years in Arabia before he was released into his assignment. God has his way of hiding us for a season to get our undivided attention and make a spiritual deposit into our lives.

> The purpose of isolation in the cave is to turn our messes into messages.

Streams in the Desert summarizes well the reason and benefit of the isolation period:

It is certainly unnecessary to say that turning conviction into action requires great sacrifice. It may mean renouncing or separating ourselves from specific people or things, leaving us with a strange sense of deprivation and loneliness. Therefore the person who will ultimately soar like an eagle to the heights of the cloudless day and live in the sunshine of God must be content to live a relatively lonely life.

There are no birds that live in as much solitude as eagles, for they never fly in flocks. Rarely can even two eagles be seen together. And a life that is dedicated to God *knows divine fellowship*, no matter how many human friendships have had to be forfeited along the way.

God seeks "eagle people," for no one ever comes into the full realization of the best things of God in his spiritual life without learning to walk alone with Him. We see Abraham alone "in the land of Canaan, while Lot lived among the cities ... near Sodom" (Gen 13:12). Moses, although educated in all the wisdom of Egypt, had to spend forty years alone with God in the desert. And Paul, who was filled with all the knowledge of the Greeks and who sat "at the feet of Gamaliel" (Acts 22:3 quoted from KJV), was required, after meeting Jesus, to go "immediately into Arabia" (Gal 1:17) to learn of the desert life with God.

May we allow God to isolate us, but I do not mean the isolation of a monastery. It is in the experience of isolation that the Lord develops an independence of life and of faith so that the soul no longer depends on the continual help, prayers, faith, and care of others. The assistance and inspiration from others are necessary, and they have a place in a Christian's development, but at times they can actually become a hindrance to a person's faith and welfare.

God knows how to change our circumstances in order to isolate us. And once we yield to Him and He takes us through an experience of isolation, we are no longer dependent upon those around us, although we still love them as much as before. Then we realize that He has done a new work within us and that the wings of our soul have learned to soar in loftier air.

We must dare to be alone, in the way that Jacob had to be alone for the Angel of God to whisper in his ear, "Your name will no longer be Jacob, but Israel" (Gen 32:28); in the way that Daniel had to be left alone to see heavenly visions; and in the way that John had to be banished to the Isle of Patmos to receive and record "the revelation of Jesus Christ, which God gave him" (Rev 1:1).[4]

The purpose of isolation in the cave is to turn our messes into messages. If God has taken you into a time of isolation, then I would encourage you to embrace this time. Allow this to be a time of receiving revelation from God that you would have never received without this time in your life.

Perhaps God has placed you in your own desert period. Perhaps you cannot make sense of the situation in which you find yourself. If you press into God during this time, he will reveal the purposes he has for you. The key is pressing into him. Seek him with your whole heart and he will be found. God may have a special calling and message he is building in your life right now. Trust in his love for you, that he will fully complete the work he has started in you.

11

STAGE 4: THE CROSS

EVERY LEADER MUST EXPERIENCE THE CROSS THROUGH BETRAYAL

If you don't pick up your cross you will be crushed by it.

—Jim Caviezel, actor, *Passion of the Christ*[1]

The fourth stage of the Joseph calling for helping to discover, navigate, and fulfill your purpose is the cross. There appears to be an unwritten spiritual law that God requires of leaders that he uses significantly in his kingdom. I call it *the graduate level test*. This test contributes more to a leader coming to his own personal cross than any other activity.

Many who have matured in their faith journey needed help to get to that maturity. There are certain experiences God allows that are designed to bring us to the absolute end of our carnal lives. This is so that Christ fully lives through us. Even the best of saints are unable to crucify the flesh by themselves. We might be able to put two nails into our own cross, but it always takes someone else to drive in the third one. And that usually involves some type of betrayal in the life of the leader.

Most of the great leaders in the Bible experienced some form of betrayal:

- For Moses, it was Korah.
- For Job, it was his three friends.

- For Jesus, it was Judas.
- For David, it was Absalom.
- For Joseph, it was his brothers and Potiphar's wife.

Betrayal is God's graduate level course for leaders. Joseph would have never been made prime minister of Egypt had he not passed the test of forgiveness from the betrayal of his brothers. Job would never have been restored had he not forgiven the betrayal of his three friends who wrongfully judged him. David would never have become the leader he was without the betrayal he experienced. And Jesus would never have become the Savior had he not forgiven our betrayal

> We might be able to put two nails into our own cross, but it always takes someone else to drive in the third one.

of him and taken on our sin. He also needed Judas to fulfill his role in putting him on the cross. You are nothing in the kingdom of God until you have been betrayed, until you have come to know the fellowship of Christ's sufferings. This wounding must be experienced so one can be acquainted with his grief.

There was a man who was a committed Christian who once worked on a cargo ship. He shared his faith with others and was a model worker. The captain of the ship was unmarried and sleeping with his girlfriend. One day this Christian man led the sea captain's girlfriend to Christ. The captain already hated and ridiculed the Christian worker because of his faith in Christ, but when his girlfriend came to Christ, she stopped sleeping with the captain, and so the captain blamed the Christian man for the change in his girlfriend.

One day the captain entered the restaurant where the Christian man was having lunch. He walked over to his table and began hurling obscenities and beating him. The Christian man simply tried to defend himself but did not fight back. The captain kept beating him until eventually the man lay on the floor bleeding.

Two men entered the restaurant and saw what was taking place. They jumped the sea captain and took him outside and then began beating him. He was beaten so badly that he needed immediate medical attention. When the Christian worker saw the condition of the sea captain, he came to his aid and began helping him. The captain was so moved that this man could do this after he had beaten him bloody that he began to weep, not understanding what could move a person to have such love in the face of being beaten. The captain accepted Jesus at that moment.

This is a practical story of what Christ did for each and every one of us. This man was willing to lay down his life for this sea captain, with the result that the captain gave his life to Jesus. In a similar way, Jesus responded in love when he was placed on the cross because of our sin.

The apostle Paul understood what it meant to embrace the cross. He realized it was the cross that created life for others. He wrote, "For we who are alive are always being given over to death for Jesus' sake, so that his life may also be revealed in our mortal body. So then, death is at work in us, but life is at work in you" (2 Corinthians 4:11–12).

We can also see the emotions of David as he describes a painful betrayal by someone close to him:

> If an enemy were insulting me,
>   I could endure it;
> if a foe were rising against me,
>   I could hide.
> But it is you, a man like myself,
>   my companion, my close friend,
> with whom I once enjoyed sweet fellowship
>   at the house of God,
> as we walked about
>   among the worshipers.
> (Psalm 55:12–14)

THE ROLE OF PAIN IN MATURITY

God often uses our pain to bring us to the point of the cross. He is rarely the author of it, but he uses the assaults of the devil to bring us to maturity. Until we experience our own personal cross, we will never experience the depths of God. God first gives us the cross, and then he gives us himself. Oswald Chambers suggests we often see Jesus Christ wreck a life before he saves it,[2] and Jesus said, "Do not suppose that I have come to bring peace on earth. I did not come to bring peace, but a sword" (Matthew 10:34).

> God first gives us the cross, and then he gives us himself.

Every believer is called to experience the cross. Paul admonished the Philippians in this way:

> In your relationships with one another, have the same mindset as Christ Jesus:
> Who, being in very nature God,
> did not consider equality with God something
> to be used to his own advantage;
> rather, he made himself nothing
> by taking the very nature of a servant,
> being made in human likeness.
> And being found in appearance as a man,
> he humbled himself
> by becoming obedient to death—
> even death on a cross!
> (Philippians 2:5–8)

Jesus gave us the example of a life that is lived under the cross. You and I are called to this same type of life. God will continually take you through seasons of the cross as preparation for what he has called you to do. It is a required test in order for your call to be fulfilled. These can be dark times to be certain, but they are necessary. These times of darkness do not slow you down in your journey toward him; they may seem to, but in fact they hasten you toward the final point of your journey. Jeanne Guyon, a sixteenth-century writer, explains:

> Nor will you find any comfort from man when you have been put on the cross ... . The believer who loves the cross finds that even the bitterest things that come his way are sweet. The Scripture says, "To the hungry soul every bitter thing is sweet" (Prov. 27:7).[3]

Our job is to "die"; his job is to raise us up. Roman 6:4 tells us we are to be buried with him: "We were therefore buried with him through baptism into death in order that, just as Christ was raised from the dead through the glory of the Father, we too may live a new life." There is no victory without a resurrection of our lives in Christ so we can impact the world around us. He does not want us to stay in this place. He has a plan for our lives. He has preordained the works he created for us to do (Ephesians 2:10).

HIS RESPONSE MUST BE OUR RESPONSE

Jesus does not give his followers a free pass on forgiving those who hurt us. In fact, he requires that we forgive in order to be one of his disciples. He uses some strong language for those who choose not to forgive others who have sinned against them. Jesus even tells us to be proactive toward those who spitefully use us and betray us:

> "Blessed are you when people insult you, persecute you and falsely say all kinds of evil against you because of me." (Matthew 5:11)

> "But if you do not forgive others their sins, your Father will not forgive your sins." (6:15)

"You have heard that it was said, 'Love your neighbor and hate your enemy.' But I tell you, love your enemies and pray for those who persecute you, that you may be children of your Father in heaven. He causes his sun to rise on the evil and the good, and sends rain on the righteous and the unrighteous. If you love those who love you, what reward will you get? Are not even the tax collectors doing that? And if you greet only your own people, what are you doing more than others? Do not even pagans do that? Be perfect, therefore, as your heavenly Father is perfect." (5:43–48)

I have experienced five major betrayals in my life. Thankfully, I have had the grace to forgive and even bless those who have betrayed me. God challenged me practically when one of the men who betrayed me was someone with whom I was in a business partnership. I was tempted to stop promoting his work, but then God said, *What part of bless your enemies do you not understand?* I will not say that it has been easy. Sometimes people must do things out of pure obedience, regardless of whether they feel good about it emotionally. All but one of these people have reconciled with me. In fact, one of them took five years before he was willing to reconcile.

Sometimes people wrongfully believe that they must be reconciled with those who betray them in order to be healed, that vindication is important to gain victory. But that is simply not true. The truth is that some people will never forgive you. Jesus was not vindicated; he went to the cross. Even two thousand years after his death people refuse to believe what Jesus had to say about himself. People die for their belief in him; families are split over his name.

You should know that forgiveness is as much for you as it is for your offender. Until you forgive, you will remain in a prison cell. True forgiveness of those who wrong us demonstrates more than anything else whether or not you are serious about walking with God at a deeper level. Any biblical teaching that does not lead us into applying truth that leads to a personal encounter with God only makes us religious. If we only give lip service to forgiving others, then we are living a religious, hypocritical spiritual life. Pride keeps us from forgiving others.

The bottom line is that people who hold on to unforgiveness and bitterness make themselves out to be victims and have not seen the wickedness of their own sin before the cross. Oswald Chambers tells us that "no sin is worse than the sin of self-pity, because it obliterates God and puts self-interest upon the throne. It opens our mouths to spit out murmurings and our lives become craving spiritual sponges."[4]

None of us can stand before almighty God and give a reason why we cannot forgive our offender because of the forgiveness God has extended to us through the death of his own Son on our behalf. This is pride at its greatest level. God can heal the sting of a betrayal if we take the first step toward forgiveness: it begins with recognizing our own need for mercy.

When Jesus washed Judas' feet, knowing what his disciple was about to do, it spoke volumes about what our heart must be like toward our betrayers. We can't look down on another when we are washing their feet. Love is at the core of true forgiveness.

THE POWER OF FORGIVENESS

Loving someone who does not deserve it has an incredible impact on the betrayer. The Bible tells us it is like putting hot coals on that person's head: "If your enemy is hungry, feed him; if he is thirsty, give him something to drink. In doing this, you will heap burning coals on his head" (Romans 12:20).

The true gospel is faithfulness expressed in the face of unfaithfulness. People often develop their theology based on the level of pain-avoidance and lifestyle they want, instead of on what the Bible teaches.

I have a close friend who was the CEO of a publicly traded company and was serving as a spiritual gifts pastor at his church. But he lived a double life for several years, which almost led him to commit suicide. By the grace of God, God spared his life. He finally went to his wife to confess his sin, fully expecting her to divorce him. Her response was beyond human comprehension.

> When we are forced into a battle we did not choose, it is the place of initiation to live for a cause greater than ourselves.

She was deeply hurt and felt the pain of betrayal, but she forgave him right on the spot. When asked about why she could have the grace to forgive her husband so quickly, she said, "I loved my husband more than anything despite everything he has done, and I knew that God would help us get through this hard situation. I had made a promise to God and my husband to be married to him as long as we were both alive, and it wasn't an option to break that promise. I need daily forgiveness for all of my mistakes; how can I expect God and others to forgive me if I am unwilling to forgive anyone, and especially someone with whom I share my life?"

When we are forced into a battle we did not choose, it is the place of initiation to live for a cause greater than ourselves. It is in this battle where we learn the reality of our faith and whether the God we intellectually believe in can be trusted with the outcome of our lives. Light is meant to shine in the darkness; the greater the darkness, the greater the impact that light has upon that darkness.

Everyone must come to a place where they know and experience what they believe. For many, this becomes the launching pad for a deeper faith experience and advancement toward their larger story. But for others it becomes a crossroads for a shipwrecked faith. They become the victims to their crisis and to unforgiveness instead of becoming victors. Oswald Chambers describes the death process in this way:

They that are Christ's have crucified the flesh—it is going to cost the natural in you everything, not something. Jesus said—"If any man will be My disciple, let him deny himself," that is, his right to himself, and a man has to realize Who Jesus Christ is before he will do it. Beware of refusing to go to the funeral of your own independence. The natural life is not spiritual, and it can only be made spiritual by sacrifice. If we do not resolutely sacrifice the natural, the supernatural can never become natural in us.[5]

That is to say that there can be no triumph without loss, no victory without conflict, no peace gained without a crisis. God shakes *that* which can be shaken. Someone suggested that it is only a crucified person who can have fellowship with a crucified Lord.[6]

Walking successfully through your season of the cross gives you the authority to minister the message God deposits into you and to fulfill the purpose for which God created you. The level of adversity corresponds to the level of the call and the depth and width of the ministry and purpose he plans through your life. If you are to be used to impact many people, then God will take you through a greater level of testing and scrutiny in order to create a level of holiness that is commensurate with your calling.

If your foundation is not solid, then satan will pick you off as you scale any mountain of influence. Joseph's preparation would seem to be extreme; however, it was that level of preparation that allowed him to rule for eighty-one years at the top of a governmental mountain.

The farther we travel on our spiritual journey, the less responsive God seems to our requests for a pleasant life. Theologically, this statement may not be accurate, but it simply *seems* that way at times. When I was a young believer, it seemed my prayers were answered immediately, but now that I am much older and mature in my faith, it seems that God's response is simply not the same. He seems to leave me to work things out before I see his hand move.

This can be a dangerous place for us if our faith is not grounded in the belief that God is love and his motivation is always for our good. One of the best ways to shipwreck our faith is to focus on what God is not doing versus what he is doing. If we are not careful, then we can impugn the nature of God because he is not responding the way we think he should be.

If God calls us into darkness in order to enter his presence, then that darkness will become an entry to new levels of relationship with a God who longs for fellowship with us. The devil does not want me to succeed; however, my goal is for the devil to see me as a lost cause. I want him to fear every day when I put my feet on the floor. I want him to know I am a major threat to the kingdom of darkness. It is my desire that there would be a "Wanted" poster in hell with my name on it so that demons recognize I am one of their greatest threats!

Jesus never got flustered about any crisis in which he entered. He already knew there was a solution to each of them. So too must we believe. Don't let your circumstances change your faith; let your faith change your circumstances. Remember, visions make leaders passionate, but thorns keep them authentic. Even satan's schemes against us can be used for fertilizer for greater growth; adversity is often the manure for spiritual growth. God is looking for those he can entrust a problem to who will manifest a God-given solution to that problem.

Staying the course is important as we walk out the Christian life. Sometimes we must fight through times of the cross. Oswald Chambers says, "When God puts the dark of 'nothing' into your experience, it is the most positive something He can give you."[7]

Our level of maturity is often revealed by what causes us to lose peace. The temptations that come with prosperity are far greater than those that accompany adversity. The depth of your cross experience determines the degree of fruit that will come from your life. Chambers goes on, "No matter how disagreeable things may be, say—'Lord, I am delighted to obey Thee in this matter,' and instantly the Son of God presses to the front and in our human minds there is formed the way of reasoning that glorifies Jesus."[8]

Let's face it—a dead person can't have stress. Satan's goal is to badger us right out of the presence of God. But adversity is God's tool to loosen our desire for this world and motivate us to seek him and embrace him for the solution to every need. Sometimes subtraction comes before addition, dismantling before remantling. And Paul wrote, "We were therefore buried with him ... that, just as Christ was raised from the dead ... we too may live a new life" (Romans 6:4).

Oswald Chambers explains the cross in this way:

> No one experiences complete sanctification without going through a "white funeral"—the burial of the old life. If there has never been this crucial moment of change through death, sanctification will never be more than an elusive dream. There must be a "white funeral," a death with only one resurrection—a resurrection into the life of Jesus Christ. Nothing can defeat a life like this. It has oneness with God for only one purpose—to be a witness for Him.[9]

What Is the Goal of the Christian Life?

The goal of the Christian life is death. Our old nature must die so Christ may live through us! This is for every believer: "Then Jesus said to his disciples, 'Whoever wants to be my disciple must deny themselves and take up their cross and follow me. For whoever wants to save their life will lose it, but whoever loses their life for me will find it'" (Matthew 16:24–25). One day a mentor said to me, "I would kill you myself if I could." I was struggling to get past my own stuff. I was trying to birth something that only God could birth by embracing the cross.

The Christian life is often a paradox: die to live, give to receive, be last in order to be first, death to gain life, go low to go high, and give to receive—God's economy is different than ours. We all need to have a funeral before we can experience true life in him. We all must die quietly. *Dead* people don't have to protect their reputations—God does it for them.

We all need to remember that when God wants to achieve great influence through a life, he permits great challenges. Those challenges are God's ways for achieving great destinies. Is someone in your life trying to put the third nail into your death process? Do not fight it. Allow God to complete his process.

"Precious in the sight of the LORD is the death of his faithful servants. ... You have freed me from my chains" (Psalm 116:15–16). When there is death, there is new life and freedom for the believer. Michael Molinos summarizes spiritual death for the believer when he writes, "Doing is delightful. It belongs to beginners in Christ. Suffering belongs to those seeking. Dying—dying to the self—belongs to those who are being completed in Christ."[10]

Friend, if you've never asked God to crucify all that is in you that is not of him, then let me encourage you to pray that prayer right now. Death in our old nature creates the new life in Christ we all should desire. If there are those you need to forgive, why not do it right now? Here is a suggested prayer:

Father, today I want to forgive _____. I no longer hold them in debt to me for the sin they committed against me. I acknowledge that I, too, am a sinner in need of forgiveness. I choose to forgive them because you forgave me. Thank you that life begins with death to my old nature. I pray that you will crucify my old nature today so Christ can live completely through me. In Jesus' name I pray. Amen.

STAGE 5: PROBLEM SOLVING

You Are Called
to Solve a Problem

No individual has any right to come into the world and go out of it without leaving behind him distinct and legitimate reasons for having passed through it.

— George Washington Carver[1]

The fifth stage, the problem-solving stage, is a key component of the six stages of the Joseph calling. Once God has taken you through a process of maturity, then the fruit of that process often results in you solving some type of problem that ultimately gives you the authority in which God wants you to operate.

For example, God raised up Pharaoh in order to demonstrate his power to him, his nation, and the people of Israel (Romans 9:17). Through Moses, God solved the problem of freeing the people of Israel from slavery, using as the catalyst a series of miraculous plagues. This is how God works through us to bring solutions that can solve problems in our world. We gain influence by being better and by providing solutions to culture's leaders and their problems. And when there are injustices, we tap into the power of God for the solution to the injustice, just as Martin Luther King Jr. did. It may cost you your life when you stand up for righteousness and a cause that is bigger than yourself.

An Inventor Solves a Problem

Johannes Gutenberg was a German goldsmith and inventor best known for inventing the Gutenberg press in 1455. God gave him the skill to create what may well be the most important invention of all time when its impact is measured on the larger culture. Listen to the passion of this man whom God used to change the world through his invention:

> Religious truth is imprisoned in a small number of manuscript books which confine instead of spread the public treasure. Let us break the seal which seals up holy things and give wings to Truth in order that she may win every soul that comes into the world by her word no longer written at great expense by hands easily palsied, but multiplied like the wind by an untiring machine.[2]

It appears that some people questioned the value of Gutenberg's invention, which is nothing new for those whose ideas often have a significant impact on the world. But Gutenberg understood the value of the gift God had allowed him to create, and so he stated:

> Yes, it is a press, certainly, but a press from which shall flow in inexhaustible streams the most abundant and most marvelous liquor that has ever flowed to relieve the thirst of men. Through it, God will spread His Word; a spring of truth shall flow from it; like a new star it shall scatter the darkness of ignorance and become a cause of light hitherto fore unknown to shine among men.[3]

I find the timing of Gutenberg's invention extraordinary. It seems that God preordained this invention for what was to come just fifty-seven years later. That would be the year 1517, when Martin

Luther would nail his Ninety-Five Theses to the Wittenberg door, which would be the catalyst that would usher in the Protestant Reformation. Gutenberg's press printed and circulated Luther's writings throughout Europe, and printed a Bible in the native language of Germany. Truly, this was God's invention for humanity but it was created by a businessman. No other invention has had a greater impact on humankind as the printing press. The Word of God began to reach the common person for the first time because of his press.

When Billy Graham was asked where he saw God moving in the world today, he answered by saying:

> Back when we did the big crusades in football stadiums and arenas, the Holy Spirit was really moving—and people were coming to Christ as we preached the Word of God. But today, I sense something different is happening. I see evidence that the Holy Spirit is working in a new way. He's moving through people where they work and through one-on-one relationships to accomplish great things. They are demonstrating God's love to those around them, not just with words, but in deed.[4]

When satan throws bricks at you, let God use them to build his kingdom by tapping into heaven and letting God solve the problem.

Unfortunately, for many in the body of Christ today, people can't hear what we are saying because our negative actions are speaking louder than our actual words. Are there any actions that are hindering your words?

When satan throws bricks at you, let God use them to build his kingdom by tapping into heaven and letting God solve the problem. Jesus never fretted over a problem; he already has a solution. So too do you, because Jesus lives inside of you. Solving problems will give you greater authority and influence. When Jesus told the disciples to feed the five thousand, he enabled them to fulfill the assignment. God enables what he instructs us to do!

These attacks may be satan's manure, but he fails to realize that we are able to turn what he means for evil into spiritual fertilizer for breakthroughs and kingdom growth. We live in a war zone, but each battle we win takes us closer to winning the war and having more influence in the lives of others and the culture at large. We are being used to reveal heaven on earth.

Solving a Problem for Farmers

George Washington Carver is one of the greater inspirational stories of all time. Here was a man who should have been a victim to his circumstances. He lived during the worst time of slavery in America. He lost his mother to the slave trade; he was discriminated against continually. Yet he was a follower of Jesus who was gifted with an inventive mind. He discovered more than three hundred uses for the peanut that transformed the Southern economy. At the age of sixty-three, he wrote:

> Man, who needed a purpose, a mission, to keep him alive, had one. He could be ... God's co-worker. ... My purpose alone must be God's purpose. ... As I worked on projects which fulfilled a real human need forces were working through me which amazed me. I would often go to sleep with an apparently insoluble problem. When I woke the answer was there.[5]

Solving problems—whether for God, your government, your employer, or your city—raises the value of your influence capital. Increased favor is for the increased ability to serve others more effectively to build God's kingdom on earth, not our own kingdoms.

Irish statesman Edmund Burke, who lived in the mid-1700s, said, "All that is necessary for the triumph of evil is that good men to do nothing."[6] Today we live in a culture that wants to see what we are, not what we say we are. Our faith needs to be winsome so that we might win some. We need to stop telling people what we don't believe in and live out what we do believe. When we combine genuine, loving faith with problem solving, it becomes a powerful and winsome combination that invites people to learn more about the source of that motivation.

I first met Nancy Alcorn in March of 2014 at a conference in Florida. The more I learned about her story, the more impressed I was that she was an example of someone God was using to solve a problem in the lives of many young women today.

Nancy is the president and founder of Mercy Multiplied, which brings transformation to broken, troubled young ladies throughout the world. She is an author and frequently speaks at conferences in many nations. I asked Nancy to share what problem she is solving for young women today. She wrote me and shared her story.

When I first received Christ after my senior year of high school, one of the first things I said was, "Don't ever ask me to pray out loud, don't ever ask me to speak in front of a group, and don't ever ask me to give my testimony because this is going to be a private thing with me." To me, it was unthinkable that I could stand up in public and talk about God, but He had other plans.

During and after college I worked for the state of Tennessee. Working in a correctional facility for juvenile delinquent girls and then for the Department of Human Services investigating child abuse cases, I was touched by the broken lives I came in contact with on a daily basis. Although those eight years of working for the state gave me invaluable experience, they were extremely frustrating years for me. The one thing that became very clear to me during this time was that God has not anointed the government to heal broken hearts and set captives free, but God has called His people to do it (see Isaiah 61:1). Neither the government nor any other secular program can ever bring the lasting change that these young women need, because it is only through Jesus Christ that they can be given a new heart and a new spirit.

While I worked for the state, I volunteered many hours with the local Teen Challenge center, working with troubled girls. I would go to work for the government during the day not having the freedom to share about the One I knew could change lives. But during my off hours, I was able to volunteer at Teen Challenge with the full freedom to share Christ with the girls. It was there I began to see young girls set free from addictions through the power of Christ. In the state setting, the experts called addiction a disease and said you could never be free. However, with the freedom to share the truth of God's word in a Christ-centered Teen Challenge environment, I began to see young girls set free from addictions.

Eventually, Teen Challenge offered me a full-time position, and I was appointed Director of Women for the first girls' home where I served for two years. During this time of working with young girls with addictions, I received a deeper revelation of how Christ was the answer to every problem, not just addictions. I began to be moved with compassion toward young girls facing eating disorders, unplanned pregnancies, sexual abuse, suicidal tendencies, and depression. What God was showing me was that if the name of Jesus is above every name, and that Christ can set us free from anything and make us new, then why just addictions? I truly developed a passion for reaching hurting young women with the unconditional love and forgiveness of Jesus Christ.

In January 1983, God directed me to move to Monroe, Louisiana, to establish the Mercy Multiplied program. The vision for this program was to establish a faith-based residential facility for girls ages thirteen to twenty-eight with all kinds of problems and issues. God instructed me that if I would do three specific things, then He would always see to it that our needs would be met: 1) take girls in free of charge so they do not think we are using them to make money off their problems, 2) tithe at least 10 percent of all the money that comes in to other Christian organizations and ministries, and 3) do not take state or federal funding, or any other money with strings attached, where we would not have the freedom to share about Jesus Christ. Since 1983 we have continued to be faithful to these three principles and God has been true to His Word and faithful to provide every need.

Mercy Multiplied began with a small facility, and after adding on twice, we began to see the need for an additional home to make room for more unwed mothers. In 1987, we stepped out in faith, believing for God to build this home debt-free. After several months of building, the contractor told me that we would need an additional $150,000 to complete the project. It was at this point that we made the decision to sow our last $15,000 in the building fund as a seed for what we needed.

A few weeks later, God arranged for a divine appointment on an airplane that proved to be a major turning point. I had just spoken at a week-long evangelism conference in Las Vegas and was exhausted, the last man to board the plane sat down in the seat next to me and began a conversation by asking how much money I had lost gambling during my trip to Vegas. I explained to him my purpose for being in Vegas and of my commitment to Christ. The man was so amazed that someone would come to Las Vegas and not party and gamble that he began asking questions about what I do for a living. It was at that point that I shared with him about the work of Mercy Multiplied.

The man then began to tell me his story. He had been born to a teenage mother who had been violently raped; he was a product of that rape. Because people were there to help his mother get the help she needed, she chose life and placed him up for adoption when he was five days old, and he was just sure that if his mother had not had a place to go, a place like Mercy Multiplied, he would have been aborted. His adoptive mother, whom he had dearly loved, had recently passed away and left him with several million dollars. As I listened intently, he told me that he had been looking for something to do in memory of his adoptive mother. He asked me how much more money we would need to compete the building. When I told him that $150,000 was still needed, he simply replied, "You've got it."

God provided for us then, and has continued to provide for every need over the years. He is faithful to His Word, and when we get involved in reaching hurting people with the unconditional love of Christ, it is then that Jehovah Jireh, our provider, will jump right in the middle of what we are doing to make sure that every need is met.

Currently, Mercy Multiplied has multiple locations in America and in six other nations around the world. We have plans underway for many more locations both in the United States and abroad. Mercy Multiplied is a testament of what God can accomplish through our obedience to His will. I never imagined that God would use me to establish a vision of hope that would reach so many people. I encourage you, in the face of fear or lack, to be obedient to what God has put in your heart to do, and follow Him fully as you take the steps of faith that will lead you into the fulfillment of your dreams, amazing things happen and lives are changed when we are willing to seek His anointing on our lives and say Lord, "Here am I! Send me."[7]

How Did Jesus Solve Problems While He Walked on Earth?

Dear friends, do you think you'll get anywhere in this if you learn all the right words but never do anything? Does merely talking about faith indicate that a person really has it? ... Isn't it obvious that God-talk without God-acts is outrageous nonsense? (James 2:14, 17 MSG)

Often our efforts to bring change to our world (even within conservative Christianity) has led to manipulation, domination, and control. When God told the Israelites in Deuteronomy 8 that they would be the head and not the tail, this would be the fruit of their obedience by fulfilling the first and greatest command, which was to love and obey God. It was not a goal to try and achieve dominion over the rest of the world. Rather, it was the fruit of their obedience that would bring real change.

Looking at the life of Jesus, we can see his strategy used to influence the life of an individual. His life and actions did not always lead to impacting the broader culture, but he did impact the community of Samaria. When Jesus ministered to a Samaritan woman, for example, she was impacted and went inside the city to tell everyone about him. In fact, John tells us Jesus stayed in that city and many believed in him. This was one of the first cities impacted broadly by Jesus: "Many of the Samaritans from that town believed in him because of the woman's testimony, 'He told me everything I ever did.' So when the Samaritans came to him, they urged him to stay with them, and he stayed two days. And because of his words many became believers" (John 4:39–41).

Another strategy that Jesus employed was that he crossed the barrier of social norms. Customs of the day said that Jews did not speak to Samaritans, especially to a Samaritan woman. "Just then his disciples returned and were surprised to find him talking with a woman. But no one asked, 'What do you want?' or 'Why are you talking with her?'" (John 4:27). Jesus crossed these social boundaries and spoke to anyone who needed to hear the good news.

There is a tendency in the Christian community to isolate ourselves from those who think and believe differently than us. We believe that if we are befriending someone who might believe or live another type lifestyle, then we are endorsing that lifestyle. But Jesus did not think that way. He realized he came to save those who were lost.

Oswald Chambers said, "It is not a question of being saved from hell, but in being saved in order to manifest the Son of God in our mortal flesh."[8] Jesus didn't save us solely to take us to heaven; rather, he left us here to influence the world. Jesus came to earth to solve a problem. He came to be the payment for sin and to extend an invitation of salvation through his death on the cross (John 3:16). And secondly, in Luke 19:10 (NKJV), it says, "For the Son of Man has come to seek and to save that which was lost," and to reestablish his kingdom on earth (Matthew 6:10) by giving humanity authority as his representative (28:18). Notice that in Luke 19:10, it does not say "all *who* were lost." His death was to restore all that had been lost as a result of the sin of Adam and Eve.

Jesus became a problem solver by listening to and doing the will of the Father. He only solved problems the Father told him to solve—healing the sick, multiplying five loaves and two fish, telling Peter to cast his net on the other side of the boat, and so on. It is true that Jesus solved problems in peoples' lives. The more he did this, the more his reputation spread and the more influence he had among the people and the culture. His core method was through extravagant unconditional love, servant leadership, and being led by his Father. He lived to please the Father.

This is the model we are to emulate today. The more we are like Jesus, the more influence we will have in our culture. It will happen naturally. This is one reason that Christianity is not impacting the world to the extent it could be—we as the body of Christ are failing to be problem solvers in our world.

CAN YOU BE TRUSTED WITH A PROBLEM?

Our world is moving further and further away from the spiritual foundations that have made our nation the greatest nation on earth. We will never return to that foundation unless we do what Jesus said. Instead of complaining about our status or the ungodly leaders in our country, we must begin to think differently. When a problem arises, we need to think, *How does God want to solve this problem through me?*

> Culture does not care who solves the problem; the people just want their problems to be solved.

Culture does not care who solves the problem; the people just want their problems to be solved. When we approach problems in this way, we will begin to live the model for problem solving that Jesus showed us through his own life. Can God trust *you* with a problem?

Mother Teresa was a problem solver, but she was also an activist. She gained an international voice for the down-and-outs of society by serving them. I'll never forget the speech of this ninety-pound woman standing before the United Nations, rebuking them for their failure to care for the poor. There is a time to stand as God's representative once you've earned the right to speak.

The same could be said for South Africa's Nelson Mandela, who solved a problem for South Africa by destroying apartheid in his nation. He spoke words of forgiveness and reconciliation for a people who had been ill-treated. No one had been more ill-treated than he after spending twenty-seven years in prison. That became his authority to solve a major problem in his country. Mandela said, "If you want to make peace with your enemy, you have to work with your enemy. Then he becomes your partner."[9]

God's problem solvers are men and women who solve societal problems. Young David went from delivering lunch to delivering a nation by solving a major problem for King Saul when he volunteered to fight Goliath. And there have been many such problem solvers in history. Do you want to have greater influence in your workplace, city, or nation? Then find a major problem and solve it. The fruit of those actions will be influence.

13

STAGE 6: NETWORKS

GOD WORKS THROUGH UNIFIED NETWORKS TO BUILD HIS KINGDOM

I am a strong individualist by personal habit, inheritance, and conviction; but it is a mere matter of common sense to recognize that the State, the community, the citizens acting together, can do a number of things better than if they were left to individual action.

—Theodore Roosevelt[1]

The sixth stage of the call of God in the life of a leader involves networks. One of the great values of God we see in the Scriptures is the need for groups of people to come together in unity for a cause greater than any single person could accomplish alone.

God reveals this value for unity in diversity in the Trinity—Father, Son, and Holy Spirit. Each member of the Trinity has a particular role to play. And when Jesus decided to start his worldwide mission, he recruited twelve disciples to accomplish this task. Interestingly enough, these were recruited from average men from the marketplace, not from the clergy of the day. Jesus spent three years pouring into these men and building unity among them for a common mission.

Not only that, but Daniel had a small group of men he relied on to share the burdens they had as people living in Babylon serving an ungodly king. When Nebuchadnezzar told Daniel that he had to tell him his dream and interpret it or else he would die, Daniel immediately went to his core circle of friends—Shadrach, Meshach, and Abednego—to pray together. God answered their prayer, and Daniel's life, and the lives of the men in his administration, were spared. God's name was uplifted in the whole kingdom as a result of this miracle.

We see the value of stage six of the Joseph calling already in place in Daniel's life. He had a network of covenant relationships he could go to: Shadrach, Meshach, and Abednego were prayer and covenant partners with Daniel. Their lives were threatened when King Nebuchadnezzar threatened to kill all the magicians, including Daniel and his friends, if they were not able to interpret the king's dream (Daniel 2:3–5).

When Daniel heard of the death decree, he asked for more time. He immediately went to his *network* so they could pray and seek God's mind on the matter. Daniel acknowledged that God indeed answers prayer when he proclaimed, "He reveals deep and hidden things; he knows what lies in darkness, and light dwells with him" (v. 22). God answered and saved him and his friends; the ungodly magicians were also saved. As a result of Daniel solving the king's problem (stage five), not only were his and others' lives spared, but also he and his friends were elevated and gained more influence in the government.

Daniel is a perfect example of a servant of God in government who affected change at the highest level as a result of his relationship with God. God worked through Daniel, but Daniel was also good at what he did: "In every matter of wisdom and understanding about which the king questioned them, he found them ten times better than all the magicians and enchanters in his whole kingdom" (Daniel 1:20). Are you ten times better at your job than other workers? If we are going to be effective networkers, then we must be better than our ungodly counterparts.

WILLIAM WILBERFORCE
AND THE CLAPHAM GROUP

One of the most noteworthy groups that made a difference in a society was the Clapham Group, a group of Christian influential like-minded leaders connected to the Church of England. They were social reformers based in Clapham, London, at the beginning of the nineteenth century, with William Wilberforce, an aristocrat who came to Christ at twenty-eight years of age, as their leader. His good friend John Newton, who was a converted slave trader and author of the famous hymn "Amazing Grace," convinced him to stay in politics to model his faith in the public sector. Wilberforce's life was filled with one moral and religious project after another over a forty-year period.

In 1787 Wilberforce came into contact with Thomas Clarkson and a group of antislavery trade activists, including Granville Sharp, Hannah More, and Lord Middleton. They persuaded Wilberforce to take on the cause of abolition, and he soon became one of the leading English abolitionists. The Clapham Group, as they came to be known, were mostly evangelical Anglicans who shared common political views concerning the liberation of slaves and the abolition of the slave trade, as well as the reform of the penal system in England.

The group got involved in publishing and became prominent writers and even used the creative arts to promote abolishment of slavery, which included a minted coin that contributed to the campaign. After many decades of work, both in British society and in Parliament, the group saw their efforts rewarded with the final passage of the Slave Trade Act in 1807, banning the trade throughout the British Empire and, after many further years of campaigning, the total emancipation of British slaves with the passing of the Slavery Abolition Act in 1833. They also campaigned vigorously for Britain to use its influence to eradicate slavery throughout the world.

The Clapham Group was so effective that they were described as the "spirit of the age" in England for the various reforms they achieved, including the development of Victorian morality through writings, societies that were formed, and their influence in Parliament. They were also generous philanthropists.[2]

Richard Gathro, author of an article on Wilberforce and the Clapham Group, states that this circle of friends can best be remembered by the following characteristics:

- They shared a common commitment to Jesus Christ and a clear sense of calling.
- They were committed to lifelong friendship, and mutual submission was the norm.
- Their advocacy was marked by careful research, planning, and strategy.
- They worshiped both privately and publicly, gathering twice weekly at the Clapham Church.
- Their friendships were inclusive and focused on the essentials. For example, Wilberforce was a Wesleyan and his closest friend, Henry Thornton, was a Calvinist.
- They made family life a clear priority and delighted in one another's marriages and children.
- They kept the "long view" on completing projects. Abolition of the slave trade took more than twenty years!
- They made no dichotomy between evangelism and social action. Their magazine, *The Christian Observer*, exemplifies this.
- Their faith was integral to all of life—family, career, friendship, and more. It was a faith that the younger generation calls 24-7. They talked together of a faith that impacted every part of their lives. There were no separate "compartments."

- They enabled one another versus trying to "have it all." They recognized their passions and supported one another in addressing them.[3]

The historian Sir Reginald Coupland wrote on the communal strength of the Clapham Group:

It was a remarkable fraternity—remarkable above all else, perhaps, in its closeness, its affinity. It not only lived for the most part in one little village; it had one character, one mind, one way of life. They were mostly rich, living in large roomy houses; but they all were generous givers to the poor. Thornton indeed gave away as much as six-sevenths of his income till he married, and after that at least a third of it. They could mostly have been of leisure; but they all devoted their lives to public service. They were what Wilberforce meant by "true Christians."[4]

Richard L. Gathro, in an article published about Wilberforce, explains that "he could not have done what he did without his circle of friends. Most of the books and articles written about him throughout history often overlook this critical factor;" Gathro went on to write:

One only needs to read the 400-plus letters to and from Wilberforce located in the Duke University library to begin grasping this insight. For example, it was Wilberforce's circle of friends who shared his deep faith in Christ, particularly Hannah More, who encouraged him to write a "manifesto" of what had taken place in his life and what he regarded as the essentials of the faith. The lengthy title was *A Practical View of the Prevailing Religious System of Professed Christians in the Higher and Middle Classes in This Country Contrasted with Real Christianity*. The book was an immediate success without precedent, with sales of 7,500 copies in the first six months. By 1826, fifteen editions had been printed in Britain and twenty-five in the United States. Translations of the work were printed in French, Dutch, Italian, Spanish and German. This publication served as an excellent means of expressing conviction in a society whose courtesies of life and forms of society prevented much verbal expression of religious sentiment.

The Clapham Group believed that they were representatives of God's kingdom on earth and the faithful stewards of all God had given to them. Together, this Clapham fellowship sought to make the British Empire an instrument of social and moral welfare to all people. Throughout their time together, they remained remarkably committed to these goals. The labels "Clapham Sect" and the "Saints" were given to them by others, the latter by members of Parliament.

The group had many distinctive characteristics. It had no exclusive membership requirements. They gathered together by virtue of their faith in Jesus Christ, love for one another, and out of concern for a variety of moral, social, and religious causes.[5]

The love of God was the center of the group's reason for being together and what became their legacy. From this love sprang a group that changed history. May there be many such associations that come to pass in these days as we are in desperate need of change agents in our own culture.

The Power of Moving as One

God revealed that there is incredible power in a unified vision of one group of people: "The LORD said, 'If as one people speaking the same language they have begun to do this, then nothing they plan to do will be impossible for them'" (Genesis 11:6). We usually cite this verse when describing the sin of the people trying to achieve something without God. However, God tells us that there is great power in a unified voice.

An old saying goes, "There is strength in numbers." Not only that, but Scripture tells us five will chase a hundred, but a hundred will chase ten thousand (Leviticus 26:8). "Though one may be overpowered, two can defend themselves. A cord of three strands is not quickly broken" (Ecclesiastes 4:12). And again, Deuteronomy 32:30 reminds us, "How could one man chase a thousand, or two put ten thousand to flight?"

There is a dynamic multiplication factor in unity of numbers. The Middle East saw this when hundreds of thousands gathered to stand for democracy in 2011 in Cairo, Egypt. We are a hundred times more effective when we are a unified group. In fact, a group of committed believers in the marketplace can make a difference, not only locally, but even in a nation, which is desperately needed today. James Davison Hunter, author of *To Change the World*, tells us, "The key actor in history is not individual genius but rather the network and the new institutions that are created out of these networks. And the more 'dense' the network—that is, the more active and interactive the network—the more influential it could be."[6]

> In fact, a group of committed believers in the marketplace can make a difference, not only locally, but even in a nation.

DAVID'S MIGHTY MEN

The story of David is the story of a young man who became successful as God thrust him into the larger story of his life through his defeat of Goliath before the entire nation of Israel. His life was forever changed. However, sometimes success brings other challenges when there is an insecure boss, in this case, like king Saul.

The more success and blessing that David received from God, the more Saul's fear and insecurity and jealousy grew. This eventually led to Saul opening himself up to an evil spirit that would reign in him, which led to killing God's priests. He went on seeking to murder David for many years. His insecurities, his need to be in control, and David's fame were more than he could handle. Like many leaders today, those who do their jobs well become targets of those who are jealous of their successes.

David was forced to flee from King Saul to avoid being killed. It was a low point in his life. David had to pass through Gath when he escaped, which was the city where Goliath was from. David knew the only way he could pass through Gath without being killed was if the king thought he was not a threat to him at all. How did he do this? He faked madness so the king would not think he was a threat. David must have been a pretty good actor, because his plan worked. He passed through Gath and landed in a cave called Adullam.

David must have pondered his life's circumstance as he was alone in the cave. He must have looked out over the countryside and thought, *How did my life get to this place? What happened to that prophecy from the prophet Samuel that said I was going to be the next king of Israel?* Sometimes we can come face-to-face with circumstances that seem contrary to the nature of God. We are tempted at this point to ask, *God, have you left me? Where are you in this circumstance?* One of the best ways to shipwreck our faith is to focus on what God is not doing versus what he *is* doing.

David was alone in the cave. His perception was that life had gone wrong after it had such a great beginning. Was this all there was? Let's see what happens next.

David left Gath and escaped to the cave of Adullam. When his brothers and his father's household heard about it, they went down to him there. All those who were in distress or in debt or discontented gathered around him, and he became their commander. About four hundred men were with him.

From there David went to Mizpah in Moab and said to the king of Moab, "Would you let my father and mother come and stay with you until I learn what God will do for me?" So he left them with the king of Moab, and they stayed with him as long as David was in the stronghold.

But the prophet Gad said to David, "Do not stay in the stronghold. Go into the land of Judah." So David left and went to the forest of Hereth. (1 Samuel 22:1–5)

David responded to the hand dealt to him by turning his lemons into lemonade. He worked with those dysfunctional men by turning them into what later became known as David's mighty men. These men would never lose a battle; he turned them into exceptional warriors.

> Whenever you overcome life's negative circumstances, God will give you an authority to raise up others and deliver them from their life's circumstances.

Each of us are called to turn negative life circumstances into something with which God can use to build his kingdom on earth. Whenever you overcome life's negative circumstances, God will give you an authority to raise up others and deliver them from their life's circumstances. This is your payback to the enemy for the pain he has caused in your life. That is what we saw in Nancy Alcorn's story. She took women off the street and turned them into kingdom warriors, bringing healing to their lives and giving them a future and purpose for living.

We also see this in my wife Pamela's story. After overcoming a drug addiction and serving a prison sentence, she began serving women in prison. She, like David, began to invest in the down and outs of society. That became her network to serve.

The Trumpet Call for a Unified Voice

Early in my marketplace call, God placed John 17:20–23 deeply into my spirit. Let's look at it for a moment. Jesus prayed:

> "My prayer is not for them alone. I pray also for those who will believe in me through their message, that all of them may be one, Father, just as you are in me and I am in you. May they also be in us so that the world may believe that you have sent me. I have given them the glory that you gave me, that they may be one as we are one—I in them and you in me—so that they may be brought to complete unity. Then the world will know that you sent me and have loved them even as you have loved me."

In 1997 God birthed the International Coalition of Workplace Ministries, a network of workplace ministry leaders. Our tagline was "One Mission. Separate Callings. Many Alliances." This could be said about every believer in Christ. We all have a mission to bring the kingdom of God on earth; we all have unique assignments from the Lord; and we are called to walk together in fulfilling the Great Commission to bring the gospel to others and manifest heaven on earth. ICWM is no longer in existence today; others have taken on this vision as the Lord has given me a new assignment.

In the last few years I have seen a much greater openness among leaders to work together, to lay down their silo-building and competitiveness in order to affect the greater kingdom of God. I am seeing a move of God among the body of Christ in communities across America. As of this writing, there are more than three hundred communities where church leaders, marketplace leaders, and intercessors are working together to solve problems in their communities and to be the light of Jesus in a dark world.

Hopefully, as this movement matures, we will begin to change how many unbelievers view Christianity as a right-wing political action group. God is waiting for his sons and daughters to step into their true destinies (Romans 8:19).

A New Trumpet Call

God has been preparing his marketplace followers to be a part of an end-time harvest of souls. The church has been sleeping, but it is getting aroused as we see more and more of our spiritual foundations eroding. For the first time in many years, we are beginning to see the remnant have righteous anger to be part of the solution to bring God back into our nation.

> Proclaim this among the nations:
>> Prepare for war!
> Rouse the warriors!
>> Let all the fighting men draw near and attack.
> Beat your plowshares into swords
>> and your pruning hooks into spears.
> Let the weakling say,
>> "I am strong!"
> Come quickly, all you nations from every side,
>> And assemble there.
> Bring down your warriors, LORD!
> (Joel 3:9–11)

These verses are often referred to as Joel's army coming alive in the last days. But it is also a networking verse. It speaks of a people who transform their agricultural tools (workplace tools) into weapons of love for a great harvest in the last days. Isaiah declared:

> Your people will rebuild the ancient ruins
>> and will raise up the age-old foundations;
> you will be called Repairer of Broken Walls,
>> Restorer of Streets with Dwellings.
> (Isaiah 58:12)

God is doing a great work in our day and age. He is bringing together the body of Christ like never before, so we can experience the love and unity that unite us together. God is raising up a people who are dependent on each other, unified networks to build his kingdom. Josephs play a key role in bringing unified leadership around the cultural mountains of culture.

FULFILLING GOD'S CALL IN YOUR LIFE

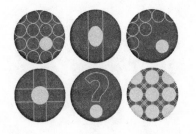

14

JACOB: FROM FAMILY SCHEMER TO NATIONAL PATRIARCH

It is a mistake to suppose that men succeed through success; they much oftener succeed through failures. Precept, study, advice, and example could never have taught them so well as failure has done.

—Samuel Smiles[1]

I f you were asked to identify with one of the biblical characters in the Bible, who would you choose? Would it be David, a man who was a worshiper of God but also had a lot of ups and downs and a great deal of failure in his life? Or perhaps it might be Abraham, who was a pioneer with great faith to step out into the unknown? Or maybe the apostle Paul, who was a strong-spirited reformer, learned in the ways of Judaism and the Law yet became a voice to the Gentiles as he traveled the world preaching the gospel. Or maybe you would identify with Esther, a beauty queen who put her life on the line, using her influence to save her people from annihilation? Or how about John, who was known as Jesus' best friend, the guy who laid his head on Jesus' shoulder?

It is good for us to identify with those who seem to reflect characteristics of our own lives and see how they lived out their faith. For me, I identify most with Jacob. Jacob came from a family that probably was not too touchy-feely. He was a momma's boy.

He exhibited insecurity that led him to manipulating others and becoming a supercontroller. Fear was at the root of all of these characteristics.

> Even though Jacob had character flaws, God saw something good in Jacob and began taking him through a process to deal with these traits.

However, even though Jacob had these character flaws, God saw something good in him and began taking him through a process to deal with these traits. God moved Jacob through the six stages of the Joseph calling to shake up a man full of fear, insecurity, and control in order to transform him into a man who would birth an entire nation. Jacob would have twelve sons, who would become the nation of Israel.

CRISIS BEGINS AT HOME

Jacob's crisis stage began with his brother, Esau. Jacob revealed one of his worst character traits when he schemed to manipulate his father into giving him the blessing of the birthright of the eldest son. Esau had been the twin who was born first and was entitled to the birthright. Even though they were twins, these brothers were quite different in personalities. Esau was a hairy young redhead who liked to hunt and fish. Jacob, on the other hand, was a mild man who dwelled in tents. He liked to read and study. Jacob was a momma's boy, but Isaac favored Esau for the game he often brought home.

Esau had a compulsive personality. He was a man focused on the here and now and on satisfying his flesh. The Scriptures tell us he sought women outside the tribe, which greatly displeased his parents. But perhaps his greatest failure was deciding to trade his birthright one day for a bowl of porridge after returning from a hunting trip. This shortsighted view would forever change the world and become part of history's greatest conflict, as is still seen today—the Jews versus the Arabs. We are still seeing the consequences of the conflict between brothers.

Jacob and his mother took advantage of an aging Isaac who could not see, and deceitfully presented Jacob as Esau, even to the extent of putting fake hair on his arms. Perhaps they felt justified in their actions because Esau willingly gave up his birthright. I have often thought of that scene and wondered why God would honor that blessing that was given under false pretense. This falls under the category of the ways of God that are beyond our limited understanding.

Jacob's actions led to a major family breach, so much so that Jacob was forced to leave his community. His mother and father sent him away to his uncle Laban's hometown in Paddan Aram. His recruitment stage, which began with a crisis, now propelled him into both stage two, which is character development, and stage three, which is isolation.

Jacob packed up and left for what was known as Haran. On the journey, however, he stopped to sleep under the stars in a place he would later call Bethel, which means "house of God." This becomes a significant night in the life of Jacob and the nation of Israel as a whole.

Bethel is located just north of Jerusalem and is mentioned in more than sixty verses in the Bible, representing more than thirty distinct Old Testament stories and prophecies. It was one of the first places in the Holy Land where the ark of the covenant of God was set up, and where the priests offered sacrifices and inquired of God (Judges 20:18, 26–28; 21:2).

The distance from Beersheba, where Jacob had been living, to Haran was more than six hundred miles. That's an incredible distance to travel through that kind of terrain, and would take an estimated 661 hours of walking. Additionally, Jacob did not take the common road, but went by lonely and unfrequented paths to avoid being sought after by Esau, which increased the length and dangers of the journey. This time of isolation must have been a time of soul-searching for Jacob. Needless to say, he had a lot of time to think.

At nightfall Jacob laid his head on a stone in Bethel and had a dream. He saw in the dream a ladder coming down to earth with angels ascending and descending on it. The Lord spoke to him in the dream and said:

> "I am the LORD, the God of your father Abraham and the God of Isaac. I will give you and your descendants the land on which you are lying. Your descendants will be like the dust of the earth, and you will spread out to the west and to the east, to the north and to the south. All peoples on earth will be blessed through you and your offspring. I am with you and will watch over you wherever you go, and I will bring you back to this land. I will not leave you until I have done what I have promised you." (Genesis 28:13–15)

Just as he had done with Abraham, God revealed the future to Jacob. He confirmed the same future he had revealed to his grandfather Abraham. He would birth a nation. Before that night at Bethel, Jacob's heart was filled with fear; afterward, he walked with a new awareness of God and his plan for his life. Before he felt the weight of his past; afterward he looked with excitement to the future. Before he was running for his life; afterward he was running to find a wife (vv. 1–4).

All of this is implied by the first phrase of Genesis 29:1 (YLT), which literally reads, "And Jacob lifted up his feet," suggesting a new spring in his step as a result of his encounter with God. Before this Jacob considered himself a fugitive, but now he had a call on his life.

This reminds me of the seven-year pit I shared about earlier. I had lost my wife to divorce, my finances crumbled, and my business was gone all within a few months. I thought life was over. Two years into my adversity, however, I met Gunnar Olson who told me I had a Joseph calling on my life that was a call to the marketplace.

That day I had my own Bethel moment. I moved from being

a victim of my circumstances to having a realization that God had a call upon my life. And I have never looked back since that time. God has since taken me to more than twenty-six countries and enabled me to write many books. He has been faithful to turn my valley of trouble into a door of hope for both me and for many others through my writing and my experiences.

After many days of traveling, Jacob arrived in Haran. He thought he would be there for a few months, find a wife, and then return home to Beersheba. Little did he know that Haran was going to be his home for twenty long years. He didn't yet know that the hard times in Haran were just the material God would use to take him through the character-building stage of his life.

Character Building at the Hands of Family

Jacob's character-building stage was largely accomplished through his manipulative uncle Laban. This guy was an idol worshiper and businessman/farmer who knew how to get the best of another person. Instead of seeing Jacob as a nephew to mentor, he used Jacob. Jacob's time of reaping from his own actions with Esau had come. For years, he had sown control and manipulation, likely through his mother, Rebekah. This was the primary character flaw God was going to work on over the next twenty years.

Laban had two daughters. Leah, the older one, was evidently not so attractive. Rachel, on the other hand, must have been a knockout because Jacob immediately fell for her. However, when he asked for Rachel's hand in marriage, Laban pulled a fast one on him. First, Laban required Jacob to work seven years for Rachel. Then, when the seven-year contract was completed and the wedding took place, Laban put Leah in the tent with Jacob. The net result was that Laban required Jacob to work another seven years in exchange for Rachel.

Jacob must have come to an understanding of his own control and manipulation as he saw himself in the actions of Laban. It is clear in the story that God had done a work in Jacob as he completed his fourteen years of service.

ISOLATION CONTINUES: "THEN JACOB WAS LEFT ALONE"

Another major turning point for Jacob came in his departure from Laban. He had been in exile from his home country, which was part of his isolation time. But he was about to have another important isolation period—not a long one but an important one nonetheless. He would be alone with the angel of God.

God gave Jacob a strategy to create large flocks from Laban's herds that was a legitimate way to allow him to be self-sustaining and allow him to leave Laban. It is worth noting here that when it's time to move into a new phase of calling, God can give you the strategy to allow you to do this. Jacob began his long trip back to the Promised Land with his family and his flocks, but met an angel along the way who informed him that Esau was coming his way. This struck fear into the heart of Jacob.

The account reveals that the breach in the relationship between Jacob and Esau lasted for more than twenty years. There had been such unforgiveness between them that neither ever made the effort to reconcile. Unforgiveness can eat at the soul of a man or woman if not dealt with. Jacob lived under the fear that Esau might take his life one day. Now, more than twenty years later, he was about to come face-to-face with his accuser. And he was scared to death.

Jacob pulled out some of his old tricks to try and appease Esau. Look at the incredible gifts he bestowed upon his twin brother:

> [Jacob] spent the night there, and from what he had with him he selected a gift for his brother Esau: two hundred female goats and twenty male goats, two hundred ewes and

twenty rams, thirty female camels with their young, forty cows and ten bulls, and twenty female donkeys and ten male donkeys. He put them in the care of his servants, each herd by itself, and said to his servants, "Go ahead of me, and keep some space between the herds."

He instructed the one in the lead: "When my brother Esau meets you and asks, 'Who do you belong to, and where are you going, and who owns all these animals in front of you?' then you are to say, 'They belong to your servant Jacob. They are a gift sent to my lord Esau, and he is coming behind us.'"

He also instructed the second, the third and all the others who followed the herds: "You are to say the same thing to Esau when you meet him. And be sure to say, 'Your servant Jacob is coming behind us.'" For he thought, "I will pacify him with these gifts I am sending on ahead; later, when I see him, perhaps he will receive me." So Jacob's gifts went on ahead of him, but he himself spent the night in the camp. (Genesis 32:13–21)

Verse 10 tells us that Jacob's nature had changed: "I am unworthy of all the kindness and faithfulness you have shown your servant." Notice the humility in Jacob here, and the truth that he says God has shown to him. Adversity and isolation times have a way of revealing truth to us like nothing else can. It can be a hard but effective tool in the hand of God.

JACOB FACES THE CROSS

Now Jacob had come to the altar of God. He entered the stage of the cross! He knew this could be it—he could die the very next day if God did not protect him and give him favor with Esau. He went to God in the night and wrestled with the angel of God. He wanted all of God. This "wrestling with God" is symbolic of Jacob's persistence to get a breakthrough. There are times in our lives where we must seek God with every ounce of energy that we have in ourselves. After wrestling with Jacob, the angel said to him, "Let me go, for it is daybreak" (Genesis 32:26). Jacob's response revealed a man desperate for God: "I will not let you go unless you bless me."

In the late 1990s, I was wresting with God. I was not getting any breakthroughs after being in my pit for almost four years. I was desperate. I wanted answers. So I decided to fast. I thought it would be a two- or three-day fast; I would not stop fasting until I felt I got an answer from God about my situation. Three days turned into six. No answers. Six days turned into ten—no answers. Ten days went to twenty, and still there were no answers. Twenty days went to thirty—still no answers! On the night of the fortieth day of a liquid-only fast, God revealed something to me.

That night was the first night of a marketplace conference with about forty other leaders. A man came to the front of the room and began to read a prophecy God had given him that day for someone attending the conference. It described my journey in detail. I met with the man after the meeting and asked him if he would pray with me about whether or not I should resurrect a failed magazine I had attempted to publish called *Christians in Business*.

We met for a time of prayer, and within five minutes the man blurted out, "God is not going to raise up the magazine, but he is going to raise up something that seems insignificant in your eyes." It turned out that what he was talking about were my devotionals, "Today God Is First." At the time, I thought they were no big deal. God had honored my persistence.

"Beware of any Christian leader who does not walk with a limp."

Jacob's encounter with God would change him forever. His name would be changed to Israel, and he would have to walk with a limp for the rest of his life because the angel dislodged it. My friend Bob Mumford used to say, "Beware of any Christian leader who does not walk with a limp." I always want to know the journey of those with whom I associate. If they have no limp, then I wonder where they are in God's development process. I live with several regrets and disappointments. This is my limp. Every day I ask for God's grace to put one foot in front of the other and to let his life be lived through my life. And so must you.

JACOB COMPLETES GOD'S PREPARATION

Jacob's life after that night of wrestling revealed that he completed the stage of becoming a problem solver. He was instrumental in establishing a people and nation that were going to be God's chosen people. His final stage, networks, can be seen in his involvement with his twelve sons, who together became the nation of Israel.

Jacob's story reveals a process by which God takes a manipulator and controller full of fear to becoming a man totally given over to the purposes of God to birth a nation. His life is so transformed that God even gives him a new name—Israel. God took Jacob from a family schemer to a national patriarch. What does God have in mind for your life?

15

MOSES: FROM ORPHAN TO WORLD CHANGER

You are never too old to set another goal or to dream a new dream.

—Les Brown

I've been fascinated by the way God invites human beings into the larger story of their lives. It's clear that every human being has a desire to count for something, to make an impact on the world in which he or she lives. As we discussed in chapters 2 and 3, there is a place in the heart of every human being to know they were created for something more. We all have a desire to connect with the heart of God's intent as to why he brought us on earth at the time and place of his choosing.

When I went through my seven years of adversity, it became a journey of self-discovery and revealed a desire to understand God's processes for his people and his activity on the earth. I first began the observation of the way God recruits his servants when I wrote my book *Change Agent*.[2] I started to look at every leader God significantly used. For most of them, the larger story of their life began with a crisis.

Then I began to recognize the additional five unique stages that often accompanied the initial crisis stage in the life of the leader. I concluded that most of us couldn't enter the larger story of our lives without the help of a significant disruption. I also noticed that this initiation into the larger story is an action brought on by either God or the devil (John 10:10).

However, even in the case of the devil's activity, God used the devil's scheme for his greater purposes by making something good out of it when a person decides to press into God in the midst of his or her crisis. The individual is often thrust into an extended time of pain, adversity, and life circumstance for an extended period that they have little ability to change. God isn't always the author of the circumstance, but he can always turn it around for good (Romans 8:28).

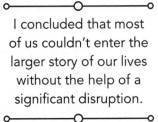

I concluded that most of us couldn't enter the larger story of our lives without the help of a significant disruption.

RECRUITMENT AND CHARACTER DEVELOPMENT

The first eighty years of Moses' life was a part of God's preparation for the work Moses would be given to do in the last forty years. During the first forty years, Moses experienced the first two stages of God's preparation for his calling—recruitment and character development. As we look at Moses' life, we can see that God recruited Moses through the circumstances of several crises. Satan tried to kill Moses at birth, but God supernaturally preserved him for a greater destiny.

During these years, God developed the godly character he wanted Moses to have. He would be put in the court of Pharaoh to learn the ways of Egypt, be educated and skilled in war, and understand a world system that he would be confronting forty years after he left. But God's more important work in Moses during this time was the development of his character while in the desert.

During this time, Moses was faced with failure when he failed to respond to adversity in unity with the will of God, and instead tried to do the will of God through the Egyptian way of the flesh. It caused him to slay an Egyptian as a means of helping the enslaved Israelites. It also led him into the third stage of God's calling—isolation.

ISOLATION AND THE LAND OF MIDIAN

As a result of Moses' failure, he spent the second forty years of his life in the Midian desert herding sheep. The Bible doesn't tell us much about Moses' time as a sheepherder, but this time of isolation was part of his preparation for the work God wanted him to do. Moses had a lot of time in the desert to be schooled by God.

Sometimes our isolation times are the first time any of us have the room for real meditation. It can be an occasion of extreme loneliness, to be sure, but that, too, is from God. It becomes a season of reflection, a time where we no longer have the comforts we once had. The isolation stage is a time of the removal where we have placed our trust. Our supports are taken from us. Modern-day isolation comes in many forms—sickness, loss of a mate, or a loss of a job. It rarely comes voluntarily as it did in the case of my good friend Colin.

BUSINESSMAN IN THE LAND OF "MIDIAN"

I first met Colin Ferreira in 2001. He had gotten ahold of my TGIF book, which resonated with him, and so he invited me to speak at an international gathering of twenty-two Caribbean Island nations in Trinidad that year. Colin was head of a marketplace ministry at the time and was the owner of the largest optical company on the island. We got to know each other really well, and he eventually joined my board, took on leadership of another international marketplace ministry in his nation, began a radio show, and headed up a national transformation initiative—oh, did I fail to mention Colin has nine kids and is in his fifties? Colin was not bored.

One day God began to share with Colin an illustration of the season he was in through a prayer intercessor. God showed him he was on a pirate ship seeking to jump off because many on the ship were trying to involve him in their organizations. But God showed up and told him to jump off because what he had for Colin's future would not be revealed through these human-made structures and

organizations. God pointed out that pirates go after legitimate treasure in illegitimate ways, and that many of God's people are going
after building his kingdom by human ways and not his own.

God began to work in Colin's heart, which led to a major life
decision. He picked up and moved his entire family to Kalona, Iowa,
a little rural community of about twenty-five hundred. This was
his wife's home area. This move meant stepping down as CEO of
his company and trusting the running of it to others. It also meant
resigning from leadership of the marketplace ministry, as well as
from the leadership team of his church, and ceasing all ministry
activities for which he had a passion.

After moving there, Colin began to question what in the
world he had done. He went from what felt like a life of extreme
purpose-filled activity to almost none at all, except for the significant roles of fathering and homeschooling his nine kids, and the
long-distance oversight of a business through some trusted man-
agers. He likened his situation to life in Midian, where Moses had
fled from Egypt.

Colin has now been in his Midian for ten years, and there have
been many times he has greatly struggled with God to understand
why he is there. He has often felt as if God has been silent with him.
He also has felt as if his life does not have meaning. He wondered
if he had been shipwrecked and whether God would ever use him
again, outside of his family.

Recently Colin and I were talking about where he was in his
life. His insights are worth noting here for those of you who may be
in your own Midian season of life:

During the first year, the move was exciting to me, as we
enjoyed many of the changes in environment and the seasons, which were quite different to the Caribbean. However,
not long after, I found myself on the proverbial hamster
wheel, spending most of my time dealing with mundane

activities arising from a still-growing family, homeschooling, and constant major repairs to a huge old house.

Almost every time when I would hire a contractor to repair something on the house, the job would be poorly done and would have to be redone by someone else. It seemed like my house was sitting on a sinkhole that was sucking away all of my time and money. I must mention that a number of years before I even considered leaving Trinidad, I was given prophetic messages that described the very house I had eventually bought in Iowa. I often wrestled with God as to why he would lead me to a house that was so problematic. I was also coming to a rude awakening that I had left a very warm culture of closely knit friendships to become part of a cold culture where very few would ever open their lives and homes to others beyond their families. The best way to describe life at this point is like being under house arrest.

For a number of years, I wrestled with depression and a sense of hopelessness. There are many elements that added to this, which would take too long to express, but the main aspects were my sense of loss of purpose and identity. Back in Trinidad I was the CEO of the leading optical company, president of the Christian chamber of commerce, host of the *God@Work* radio program, and an elder at my church. Now I am best known in my little town as Cheryl's husband. Needless to say, the assessment of being shipwrecked seemed to fit the bill.

This went on for about seven years, until God began to open my understanding of how he had completely removed the identity I leaned on and replaced it with the reality of being his beloved son. I, like most of my Christian friends and colleagues, would refer to God predominantly as "Lord," and sought primarily to serve him. I began to understand that God's primary reason for sending Jesus was to restore us to a deeply loving and engaging Father-and-child relationship.

Just like I did, I believe that most Christians live like the elder son in the parable of the prodigal son—being part of the Father's household but living like a servant because we do not know the Father whom Jesus described in the parable.

This was the beginning of a journey of fresh revelation. The best way I can think to sum up where this journey has taken me is to parallel my life with the history of the world. Humanity, in his fallen state, lived lawlessly before the law was given to Moses. Then when the law was given, he tried without success to perform the law by self-effort. Eventually, Jesus fully restores him by grace and gives him the privilege of being a son of the Father.

For me personally, there was the lawlessness before accepting Jesus as my Lord and Savior. Then there were decades of faith mixed with works and seeking to please God and build my identity through those things. Now I can say I am beginning to really understand why the gospel is called *good news*, and the extent to which we are supposed to rest in his grace and the unbreakable fellowship with our heavenly Father.

For many of us, it takes being led into a desert with nothing familiar to distract us from the things he wants to do in our lives. He is faithful. I am still in Midian, but I am beginning to smile.[3]

"Why do we often stay in our desert season so long?" This is a question I am asked a lot when I work with leaders who have gone through their own desert season. They want to know when all of this will end. I respond by saying, "It often ends when God has accomplished the deeper work in your life and the desert doesn't matter anymore."

Once we come to the place where we let go of a strong desire for something to happen, that is when God can actually move in that area. The seed must fully die in order to birth something new. The pride, the dependence on superficial stuff, and motivations for living have all been completely transformed in the life of the individual ready to leave the desert. For most of us, this process takes a considerable bit of time for all of that to be worked out. I'm often amazed by how many people I run into around the world who tell me their season in the pit was seven years, just like mine.

Let's face it—you're never going to learn to trust God with thousands of dollars in the bank. You're never going to learn to trust God when you can take a pill to solve your health problems. You are never going to seek God when you're enjoying a wonderful marriage. When you get thrown into the pit of a life circumstance, that is what will bring you to the end of yourself. That is reality. You may not see this as a gift when you are in the midst of such a season, but you will appreciate the fruit of your time there if you pass through it successfully.

The next thing that happened in Moses' journey was an encounter with a bush that was burning and talked to him (Exodus 3). God used this unusual circumstance to capture Moses' attention. God took the initiative and created a circumstance by which Moses was willing to investigate.

Once Moses got near the bush, he heard a voice that said, "Moses, Moses, take off your shoes, for you are on holy ground." God came to him during his workday as a shepherd, and the reason God told him he was on holy ground was because the presence of God was in his midst. This is an admonition to all of us, that God wants to come into the very place where we spend 60 to 70 percent of our time—our workplaces. God began to relate to Moses through the thing he was doing that day.

Then God said, "Moses, what is that in your hand?" (Exodus 4). Obviously, God knew what was in his hand, but this caused Moses to think about some things.

Moses' response to God was, "It's my staff, Lord."

God then instructed him about his calling by telling Moses to lay down his staff. When he laid it down, it turned into a snake. This was symbolic of the serpent in the garden of Eden, and Moses was now taking authority over the serpent. God told him to pick up the snake by its tail, something any seasoned shepherd knew not to do. The fact was that God was changing some paradigms! When Moses picked up the snake by the tail, the snake turned back into his staff. The Bible says that it was no longer Moses' staff, but it was now the staff of God. And it was this staff through which he would perform miracles.

A staff for a shepherd was something of great importance. Hebrew scholars tell us that the staff was used to kill snakes, poke the sheep, and, in many ways, it was a shepherd's calendar. They would etch key events in their staff and they would never have it out of their presence.

God then explained his assignment for why Moses was created and brought to the earth. Unfortunately, Moses wasn't buying it. He had a stuttering problem. He knew about the court of Pharaoh and how important it would be to be able to communicate well. His insecurities were so great that he argued with the God of the universe. That scene is humorous to me. Imagine meeting the God of the universe and you're going to argue with him about your destiny!

But we all do this, don't we? I recall when God began to inspire me to write devotionals. I was extremely insecure about the whole process. I made Cs in English class in high school, and my grammar skills were weak. When I would send these to friends via e-mail at first, I would often get responses from people with statements like, *I love your devotionals, but have you ever thought about having someone check your writing for grammar mistakes?* It was humbling to receive these e-mails.

This became a regular occurrence. It was a time when I did not have the financial ability to hire an editor, but I was compelled to share the messages anyway. Then one day an English teacher from Hong Kong asked me a similar question, and I responded by saying, "How about you?" And so he became my long-distance editor for my devotionals—for free!

I later learned from a friend who was at a major Christian publishing company that there are different kinds of writers. He said to me, "Os, there are writers and there are authors. A writer can write about anything. They are skilled at the technical side of writing. Then there are authors. Authors have something to say but need editors to help them say it. You are an author. You have something to say but simply need someone to edit your work to make it the best it can be." That input freed me to move forward in my writing.

The truth was that I was a shy person growing up. The thought of standing up in front of people and speaking simply terrified me. But that changed when the burden on my heart and the passion to share what I was learning became more important than my own comfort. I stepped into my fears, and over time God made me an effective communicator.

I'm not a flashy speaker like some, but God has given me a message that I am to share through my unique God-given personality. In fact, I find that many audiences, especially overseas, appreciate the soft-spoken nature of my personality, and they often say that I am an easy person to listen to and receive from. I have now been doing this for twenty-two years, and I have learned how to speak into the lives of others and empower them to step into the larger story of their lives.

> Sometimes we are called by God to do things that don't yield immediate fruit.

By the time Moses was eighty years old, God had invested a great deal in preparing this man to be his instrument for the deliverance of a nation from slavery. Moses failed to do one thing before he went on his journey, and God threatened to kill him over it. He failed to circumcise his son. That was important to God because it represented a covenant God made with Abraham that Moses was to maintain. This was so important to God that he threatened to kill Moses if he did not perform this act. Moses' wife saved his life by making him do it. How often has a wife saved her husband from doing the wrong thing?

God developed Moses' character as he learned to walk with God. He told Moses to tell Pharaoh to release his people, but Pharaoh refused. With each refusal came one of the ten plagues. One of the great tests of Moses' character was to be obedient to God when his obedience did not yield the fruit of deliverance, and actually made things worse for the people.

Sometimes we are called by God to do things that don't yield immediate fruit; sometimes it feels like he is actually thwarting our efforts. God did that—and does this!—in order to demonstrate to Pharaoh his mighty power. This difficult test for Moses made him a greater leader and gave him a tough skin, something we all must acquire.

Moses Faced the Cross of Stage Four

Every leader that God has used significantly has had to experience stage four of the call of God—the cross. Jesus said that unless you are willing to live as he lived, then you are not worthy to be his disciple. Living the life of Jesus means that we must pass one of the greatest tests of all, which is designed to bring every believer to a place of the cross. Many of us may say we are willing to come to the cross, as Paul describes in Galatians, "I have been crucified with Christ and I no longer live, but Christ lives in me. The life I now live in the body, I live by faith in the Son of God, who loved me and gave himself for me" (Galatians 2:20).

Even if we are personally willing to come to the cross, we can only put two nails in our own cross. God helps us become fully dead, spiritually speaking, when he sees we are willing to forgive those who have caused us great pain and may have even betrayed us. For Jesus, that betrayal came through Judas, one of the twelve disciples who walked with Jesus for three years. Jesus actually washed the feet of Judas before his betrayal.

There is something about being betrayed by those close to you that causes a level of pain that nothing else causes. There is no other way to forgive unless you come to the cross and choose to forgive your betrayer.

Moses had two major betrayals in his own life. The first was when he came down from the mountain with the Ten Commandments, he found the people making a golden calf. Aaron yielded to the pressure of the people, collected their gold, and fashioned a calf for the people to worship. However, we see the incredible response Moses had when he saw that God was going to destroy all of the people for their sin. Like Jesus, he was willing to offer himself as a sacrifice for the sins of the people:

> The next day Moses said to the people, "You have committed a great sin. But now I will go up to the LORD; perhaps I can make atonement for your sin."
>
> So Moses went back to the LORD and said, "Oh, what a great sin these people have committed! They have made themselves gods of gold. But now, please forgive their sin—but if not, then blot me out of the book you have written." (Exodus 32:30–32)

The other betrayal was the rebellion led by Korah (Numbers 16). This was also a major crisis for Moses. He felt deeply betrayed after investing so much in the people. But God judged Korah and those who rebelled against Moses by killing all of them.

If you are called to leadership, then you will have someone close to you betray you. This is in order to see if you are willing to wash the feet of your Judas.

MOSES BECOMES A PROBLEM SOLVER

God had an assignment for Moses. God invited him into a personal relationship with him. Moses would come to know God on a personal, face-to-face basis. He experienced the presence of God; he came to a place where he knew he could not even exist without God's presence in his life (Exodus 33). The Bible says he walked with God. However, the relationship ultimately led to an assignment.

God called Moses to solve a problem. The people of Israel were in slavery in Egypt. They cried out to God for four hundred years. When the time came for God to move on their behalf, he thought of one man to be his vessel to solve the problem—Moses.

God used Moses to solve many smaller problems along the way, until the larger problem was solved. He was used to demonstrate the power of God through the ten plagues; he was used to part the Red Sea to allow the people to cross over and escape the oncoming Egyptian army; he provided manna to eat while they were passing

> When God thinks of you, there is something he has in mind that you alone are uniquely qualified to do.

through the desert; God even used Moses to bring forth water from the rock. These were all smaller problems leading to the larger problem of receiving deliverance from slavery, but more importantly, entering the Promised Land.

When God thinks of you, there is something he has in mind that you alone are uniquely qualified to do. He often takes an incredibly long time of preparation it seems, but there is a moment where God often reveals the special assignment he has in mind for you. The key is to be ready when the "trumpet call" comes.

The apostle Paul heard that trumpet call when he had a dream that revealed to him what he was called to do. This is known as Paul's Macedonian call. Luke writes of it in the book of Acts:

During the night Paul had a vision of a man of Macedonia standing and begging him, "Come over to Macedonia and help us." After Paul had seen the vision, we got ready at once to leave for Macedonia, concluding that God had called us to preach the gospel to them. (Acts 16:9–10)

When God has something he wants to accomplish, he comes and speaks to us about it. Our job is to be living in such relationship with God that we can hear what he is saying and respond accordingly.

Moses' Network: The Twelve Tribes

Moses' network was the twelve tribes of Israel. Earlier I mentioned that one of the kingdom values God shows us throughout the Scriptures is the value of unity and collaboration. Moses would establish a nation through the twelve tribes of Israel. This became his network.

The key to the unbelieving world believing in Jesus is the unity of believers in Jesus Christ (John 17:20–23). God has begun a movement on the earth today, which is actually unifying his body for the times in which we live.

A Summary of Moses' Six Stages

In summary, the six stages to discovering, navigating, and fulfilling Moses' destiny are clearly seen. God recruited Moses through a crisis event: he was banned from Egypt and went Midian, and then God came to Moses at the burning bush to reveal his assignment. Moses' years in the Midian desert were part of his character-development stage. God worked with him by teaching him to obey his commands and be God's tool to release the ten plagues to show God's power. Moses was tested repeatedly by learning to lay down his life for the people of Israel; he was even willing to even sacrifice his life on their behalf.

Moses' isolation period was his forty years in the desert working as a shepherd. Then he faced the cross, where he was repeatedly challenged to lay down his life for the people of Israel. The people betrayed him when they worshiped the golden calf and when Korah led a rebellion against him.

But that was not the end of the Joseph calling on his life, the end of his destiny. God chose and used Moses to solve several problems: he needed a man to deliver the people of Israel from slavery and lead them into the Promised Land. And he did this as he networked with the twelve tribes of Israel. Through the six stages of the Joseph calling, God took Moses from an orphan to a world changer.

In a book entitled *Creative Suffering*, Paul Tournier cites an article written by Dr. Pierre Rentchnick of Geneva, which appeared in a periodical in 1975, under the surprising title "Orphans Lead the World." He went on to explain that:

> When President Ompidou died, my colleague found himself wondering what might have been the political repercussions of disease in the case of other statesmen, such as for example President Roosevelt at the end of the war. So he set about reading the life-stories of the politicians who had had the greatest influence on the course of world history (not always positive influence). He was soon struck by the astonishing discovery that all of them had been orphans! Dr. Rentchnick compiled a list of them.
>
> It contained almost three hundred of the greatest names in history, from Alexander the Great and Julius Caesar, through Charles V, Cardinal Richelieu, Queen Victoria, Golda Meir, Hitler, Stalin, Lenin, to Eva Perón, Fidel Castro, and Houphouet-Boigny to name just a few. All of these leaders suffered in childhood from emotional deprivation. So, we are giving lectures on how important it is for a child's development to have a father and a mother performing

harmoniously together their respective roles towards him. And all at once we find that this is the very thing that those who have been most influential in world history have not had! From this surprising revelation my colleague deduced 'a new theory of genesis of the will to political power': the insecurity consequent upon emotional deprivation must have aroused in these children an exceptional will to power, which drove them into a career in politics with the aim of 'transforming the world,' and succeeding in so far as they were able. Thus an unconscious will to power seems to play an important part in the lives of the most eminent men.[4]

I think of David, who was probably an orphan based on his comment in Psalm 51 that "he was conceived in iniquity." I also think of Steve Jobs, one of the great inventors of the modern era. These men made a huge impact on the culture in which they lived. Culture truly is shaped positively or negatively by early childhood experiences. So, if you are an orphan, there may be an even greater deposit of nation-changing contained inside you.

16

PAUL: FROM RADICAL RELIGIOUS TERRORIST TO DISCIPLE OF JESUS

No man is worth his salt who is not ready at all times to risk his well-being, to risk his body, to risk his life, in a great cause.

—Teddy Roosevelt[1]

I teach a lot about the principle of free will—that God gives every human being freedom of choice. God does not control us like robots. However, in reading the stories of Jonah and Paul, I must say that one could build an argument that these two guys pushed the limits of free will to the edge. God was very persuasive in changing their minds about their current plans.

Jonah spent three days in the belly of a whale to encourage him to go preach to the people of Nineveh. Paul, on the other hand, was blinded on the Damascus road, which fully got his attention and transformed him from a radical religious terrorist into a disciple of Jesus and a messenger to the Gentiles. These two examples give me hope. There are circumstances where I want God to apply pressure on me and on the people for whom I pray. Sometimes we need a strong nudge from God. I'm glad he takes a persuasive initiative in our lives to "encourage" us to make the right decisions.

A Strong Recruitment Tactic

Luke tells the story of Paul's conversion in the book of Acts:

> Meanwhile, Saul was still breathing out murderous threats against the Lord's disciples. He went to the high priest and asked him for letters to the synagogues in Damascus, so that if he found any there who belonged to the Way, whether men or women, he might take them as prisoners to Jerusalem. As he neared Damascus on his journey, suddenly a light from heaven flashed around him. He fell to the ground and heard a voice say to him, "Saul, Saul, why do you persecute me?"
>
> "Who are you, Lord?" Saul asked.
>
> "I am Jesus, whom you are persecuting," he replied. "Now get up and go into the city, and you will be told what you must do." (Acts 9:1–6)

God's approach in recruiting Saul was a strong one. He appeared to him in person, with an audible voice and a blinding light. I have traveled to the Middle East several times and I hear many stories of Jesus appearing to Muslims in dreams and visions. He is still doing the miraculous today. God desires that all people come to the saving knowledge of Jesus Christ.

So often people who have strong wills and are passionate about a cause that might be ungodly have that similar passion for the gospel once they embrace it. It is interesting that the two people chosen to lead Jesus' church were Peter, a modest fisherman with little political or financial clout, and Paul, a devout Jew who was trained under the best religious minds of the day. Paul prided himself on his knowledge and his fervor; Jesus must have known it was going to take a serious blow for Paul to reconsider his ways. What better way than to strike him blind. But Jesus was also gracious to Paul; his trauma only lasted three days.

God instructed Ananias to restore Paul's sight a few days later through a miraculous healing. This was Paul's recruitment stage:

> The Lord told [Ananias], "Go to the house of Judas on Straight Street and ask for a man from Tarsus named Saul, for he is praying. In a vision he has seen a man named Ananias come and place his hands on him to restore his sight."
>
> "Lord," Ananias answered, "I have heard many reports about this man and all the harm he has done to your holy people in Jerusalem. And he has come here with authority from the chief priests to arrest all who call on your name."
>
> But the Lord said to Ananias, "Go! This man is my chosen instrument to proclaim my name to the Gentiles and their kings and to the people of Israel. I will show him how much he must suffer for my name."
>
> Then Ananias went to the house and entered it. Placing his hands on Saul, he said, "Brother Saul, the Lord—Jesus, who appeared to you on the road as you were coming here—has sent me so that you may see again and be filled with the Holy Spirit." Immediately, something like scales fell from Saul's eyes, and he could see again. He got up and was baptized, and after taking some food, he regained his strength.
>
> Saul spent several days with the disciples in Damascus. (Acts 9:11–19)

CHARACTER BUILDING: A LIFETIME TRAINING

Jesus made a specific comment about Paul when he called him: "I will show him how much he must suffer for my name" (Acts 9:16). And did he! Shipwrecked. Imprisoned many times. Beaten and left for dead. Yet we never hear Paul complain about his plight. In fact, look at his perspective on his adversities:

We are hard pressed on every side, but not crushed; perplexed, but not in despair; persecuted, but not abandoned; struck down, but not destroyed. We always carry around in our body the death of Jesus, so that the life of Jesus may also be revealed in our body. For we who are alive are always being given over to death for Jesus' sake, so that his life may also be revealed in our mortal body. So then, death is at work in us, but life is at work in you. (2 Corinthians 4:8–12)

Paul understood that the Christian life was about death to our old nature so that the new life of Christ in us could be shared with others. He embraced his character-building process like no one else. Paul received more revelation than any other apostle, except for maybe John and Peter. He probably needed that level of revelation to endure the level of adversity he would undergo throughout his life. What I see in the life of Paul and other major influencers is that the depth and width of our adversity is often commensurate to the level of call and influence we will have.

Pain has a remarkable ability to teach us what we would never learn without this example. Our society, however, sees little worth in discovering the value of pain. Most would say it should be avoided at all costs. Larry Crabb, author of *Shattered Dreams*, writes:

We evaluate everything that happens in our life according to how it makes us feel. If we can engage in activities that directly create better feelings or, failing that, numb the troubling emotions, we do it. As long as we define our problem in these terms we will never fly. Only shattered dreams reveal the problem clearly, and only shattered dreams create a brokenness that helps us hate that attitude enough to give it up. Only shattered dreams help us feel appropriately potent.[2]

Once we gain victory over an adversity in our life, God actually gives us an authority in this area to bring healing and freedom to others. We see this in the life of Paul. His depth of writing in the epistles reveals a man who has gained deep insights into the journey through the Valley of Baka (weeping).

> Each valley becomes a spring of new revelation that is designed to equip and encourage you in your journey.

Each valley becomes a spring of new revelation that is designed to equip and encourage you in your journey. Paul's life was filled with character-building opportunities. Most came through persecution from his bold proclamation of the gospel.

REPETITIVE ISOLATION

Paul began his journey before he even met the disciples. He first entered the stage of isolation immediately following his conversion when he was isolated in the Arabian Desert for three years. There is little history on what he did there during this time. Reading Acts 9:26–28, one gets the impression that Saul went directly from his Damascus experience to Jerusalem. But by his own admission, he clarified the fact in his letter to the Galatians (1:16–17), stating, "My immediate response was not to consult any human being. I did not go up to Jerusalem to see those who were apostles before I was, but I went into Arabia. Later I returned to Damascus."

The Lord's choice for Paul was for him to go to Arabia to be trained in the school of the Spirit in order that he might receive greater revelation concerning the mysteries of the gospel of the glorified Christ. This is one of those Bible mysteries I would love to know more about. But most things written about this time are pure speculation.

Paul had other times of isolation as well, many of them spent in prison cells. It was in prison where he wrote many of his epistles. Isolation in a person's life often becomes a time of hearing God transmit a message for others. God turns messes into messages; we know for certain that Paul wrote at least thirteen letters that are included in the New Testament. No other writer was represented in the Scripture as much as Paul. Truly his isolation periods benefited millions of people through his revelation and writings.

PAUL'S CROSS: A LIFE OF REJECTION

Paul had his share of betrayals too. In his early days, his message and validity were rejected by the Jews. Even the disciples had difficulty believing this zealous persecutor of Christians was now a follower of Jesus. That became his ongoing cross. It took an act of God with Jesus appearing to Ananias before the apostles began to embrace Paul and realize his conversion was real.

In time, however, many more betrayals would follow as he fulfilled his call to preach the gospel to the Gentiles. He was a man whose call forced him to deal with rejection. When you are compelled to fulfill a mission, it does not matter how many people reject you. The mission is of greater importance than your own personal comfort.

Living a life filled with rejection is a cross some must bear. Many refuse to share Christ with the unbelieving world because they fear rejection. Yet this is a poor excuse not to share the amazing love of Christ with others. Unlike Jesus, David, and Joseph, who all experienced personal betrayal, Paul was often rejected by those who heard him preach, and even by the leadership in the early church. He often spoke of those who let him down along the way. One such case was his encounter with Mark. Luke tells of this time in the book of Acts:

Some time later Paul said to Barnabas, "Let us go back and visit the believers in all the towns where we preached the word of the Lord and see how they are doing." Barnabas wanted to take John, also called Mark, with them, but Paul did not think it wise to take him, because he had deserted them in Pamphylia and had not continued with them in the work. They had such a sharp disagreement that they parted company. Barnabas took Mark and sailed for Cyprus, but Paul chose Silas and left, commended by the believers to the grace of the Lord. He went through Syria and Cilicia, strengthening the churches. (Acts 15:36–41)

AN EFFECTIVE PROBLEM SOLVER

Jesus revealed the particular mission Paul was to fulfill through his ministry. He was to take the gospel to the Gentiles. He would be a traveling preacher, turning west toward Greece, and going even as far as Rome, as he established churches. Paul did this not only through his preaching but also through signs and wonders. His preaching was not with wise and persuasive words, but it included a demonstration of God's power working through him. If there was ever a time when the church needed signs and wonders, it is surely now. The church without power loses the validity of its message.

I have a friend who operates in the prophetic gifts. God has often revealed a detail about a person's life we were ministering to that demonstrated the power of God to that individual. On one occasion my friend spoke to a Hollywood filmmaker with the following words: "I see you have been considering suicide. I see what has happened with your wife. I see the room you are in." He continued speaking the details to him. The filmmaker was without emotion as the words were spoken. I thought my friend was off base, but hours later our host came back to us and said, "You just saved that man's life."

> If there was ever a time when the church needed signs and wonders, it is surely now. The church without power loses the validity of its message.

People don't care what you know; they want to know that you

care. And if you can be a problem solver in an individual's life, then you will have influence in that life.

PAUL'S MIGHTY NETWORK

Paul's network consisted of the many churches that he established. Paul and Barnabas became the initial tandem team, and there were other close friends and associates supporting him in his endeavors too. Priscilla and Aquila, for example, were fellow tentmakers who traveled with Paul from time to time. He could not have done what he did for the kingdom of God without a network of supporters collaborating and sharing in his vision and mission.

We can clearly see the six stages of Paul's journey reflected in his life. Each of these stages is crucial for us to discover, navigate, and fulfill the purposes of God in our own lives. If God can take Paul from a radical religious terrorist to a disciple of Jesus, then don't you think he can change your circumstances too?

17

EXPERIENCING YOUR LARGER STORY

God will not permit any troubles to come upon us, unless He has a specific plan by which great blessing can come out of the difficulty.

—Peter Marshall[1]

The purpose of the six stages of the Joseph calling is designed to usher you into the larger story of your life. That larger story should be a life that is filled with the activity of God and the manifest presence of his life being lived through you. I have lived enough years on the other side of walking through these stages that I am now seeing the fruit from successfully passing through them.

Henry Blackaby developed a popular Bible study series in 1990.[2] The premise of the study was based on seven core principles about how God relates to his people. The very first principle was that God is always at work around us; our responsibility is to join in what he is already doing. We are not to think up things to do for God; rather, we are to join him in what he wants to do and what he is already doing in the earth today. I have personally experienced this principle in many situations, and so I share these experiences to encourage your faith to see the fruit of successfully walking through the six stages of the Joseph calling.

LUNCH LEADS TO INTERNATIONAL
BANKERS' SALVATIONS

One day I received an e-mail from an American business leader living in Zurich, Switzerland, whose parents lived only a few miles from my office. Aaron Smith is a hedge fund manager in Zurich. He opened our conversation with these words: "We have a small group of leaders in the financial industry who meet for prayer and have been using TGIF for four years."

> We are not to think up things to do for God; rather, we are to join him in what he wants to do and what he is already doing in the earth today.

This was the second time I heard such a statement. I was in South Africa a few years ago and had just spoken to about a hundred men at an early morning meeting. A man came up to me after that meeting and said, "We have six TGIF groups that meet around the city."

My response was, "Excuse me! What is a TGIF group?"

"We use your TGIF devotional as a small group resource to lead our discussions. It has been great for our groups!"

After hearing both of these testimonies, I realized this was a place where God was moving. God was letting me know this was a fire he wanted me to fan by helping to form TGIF groups around the world. So we began a more intentional process to allow this to happen.

Aaron and I began to chat about what God was doing in Zurich. Then I asked him, "Did you know I was going to be in Bern, Switzerland, in October?"

"No, I had no idea," Aaron said to me.

I felt led to challenge him to host a meeting in Zurich the day before I came to Bern. I could tell this was out of his comfort zone. In many ways, this was a trumpet call moment for Aaron. When he returned to Zurich, he presented the idea to his prayer group, and they decided to embrace it.

When I arrived in Zurich, Aaron shared with me how God had taken his prayer group down this faith journey. Two weeks before the event, they had only twenty sign-ups. The venue they wanted at the UBS headquarters opened supernaturally. That night we had 145 top financial leaders come to the meeting!

Two weeks earlier I was speaking at an event in Tampa, Florida. After I spoke, the Lord gave me a download of a salvation illustration with which to close my talk. I did not know why I received it, as I had no meeting coming up for which this could be used. Then, when I arrived in Zurich, I felt led to give an invitation at the end of the meeting, as I knew there would be nonbelievers present. That was the presentation I used.

At the close of the meeting, I asked everyone to close their eyes, and I gave an invitation to these successful financial executives to invite Jesus into their lives. There were about twenty hands that went up. Aaron and his team were amazed. They had no idea God was working in their midst. However, it required them to step into a faith dimension that was not comfortable—but God honored their faith.

God Calls Us to Be Faithful in the Small Things

There is a kingdom principle that requires us to be faithful in the small areas before we are entrusted with larger ones. Jesus reminded his disciples, "Whoever can be trusted with very little can also be trusted with much, and whoever is dishonest with very little will also be dishonest with much" (Luke 16:10). This concept is also part of God's kingdom economy as it relates to finances. God's economy does not always equate to equal effort for equal pay.

Joshua 24:13 has been one of the most life-changing truths I have come to understand about God's economy. It reads, "So I gave you a land on which you did not toil and cities you did not build; and you live in them and eat from vineyards and olive groves that you did not plant." God's economy is rooted in obedience, not sweat and toil. His provision is sometimes more than I deserve and sometimes less than what I hoped for.

Several years ago, when I was going through my valley experience, money was tight. I was just starting to be invited by marketplace groups to speak at their events. A small marketplace group on the island of Barbados asked me to come and speak. My human reasoning said, *I cannot afford to spend two days with this group. The investment of time and income does not justify the effort.* Of course, God convicted me that I was to go and serve the group.

Just as I perceived, I spent two days there and the group I spoke to was only twelve people. It turned out that the primary reason I was there was to help the leader of the group, who was going through a marriage crisis. My income from the meeting was quite small. However, some of my books were left behind to share with other leaders on the island who could not attend.

A few months passed when I received a call from Colin, the man from Trinidad I wrote about earlier. He said, "I received some of your books from your trip to Barbados. They have been impactful in my life. I am hosting a conference on the island of Trinidad for twenty-two island nations. I would like you to be our keynote speaker." So I spoke at the conference and led a breakout session on the Joseph calling. One of the men who attended that session owned the largest car dealership on the islands, and he said that it was a life-changing session for him. That December I received a check for five thousand dollars from this man!

The man from Trinidad became one of my closest friends, and he still is today. He serves on my board, and we have traveled to many countries together over the last ten years. Recently I received a call from Colin, and we were talking about Trinidad. He said that abortion is currently against the law in Trinidad, but there is a movement to make it legal. He was recently in Trinidad and met a small group of Christian attorneys who were attempting to fight this legislation. Here is what he shared with me:

During my last trip to Trinidad in late April, I was invited to attend a weekly meeting of an organization in Trinidad and Tobago called Lawyers for Jesus. This is a small group of Christian judges and lawyers who have been very vocal and effective thus far in pushing back the constant attempts to have abortion legalized there (as well as other negative social issues). They have also been involved in spreading the movement to other islands in the Caribbean and mobilizing similar groups in these islands. I have been supporting them for many years, thus the reason for their invitation.

During the meeting, one of the leaders of the organization, an appeals court judge, as well as another appeals court judge, both shared with me how you impacted their lives (the appeals court in Trinidad and Tobago is the highest court in the land, similar to the US Supreme Court in our country). The first explained how she had attended the Full Gospel Business Men's Fellowship Caribbean Regional Convention in 2001. She said she had attended a workshop conducted by you, where she heard for the first time that her work was her ministry, and the lights came on for her. The other judge then explained that she had bought your book *The 9 to 5 Window* some years ago when I had bought a couple of boxes of them for my church, and it was through that book that her light came on. I was encouraged to hear this and am certain that this would encourage you also. Be blessed![3]

The fruit of the Word of God spoken into these attorneys more than twelve years ago is now being used to motivate them to make a stand against abortion in their nation.

We are called to obey God in the small areas of life. Sometimes he actually lets us see the fruit of our obedience, but at other times he does not. As we obey God in the small things, he will entrust us with the larger things, and he will cause fruit to be born from our obedience. Isaiah said this about God's Word:

> So is my word that goes out from my mouth:
>> it will not return to me empty,
> but will accomplish what I desire
>> and achieve the purpose for which I sent it.
> (Isaiah 55:11)

SOMETIMES GOD LETS US SEE OUR FRUIT

In the last several years, God allowed me to see how TGIF was touching lives around the world. I often tell people that I wrote them for me, not for others. I was simply trying to find answers, and the best way for me to do that is to study the Scriptures to find answers and write about what I am discovering. The most common comment I often get from people is, "You read my mail. You spoke right into my situation today."

Sometimes we assume God is not working when he is actually working in the most unlikely of places.

TGIF devotional is now read in more than a hundred countries and has several hundred thousand daily readers. However, readership is probably two to three times this due to people forwarding these to friends and associates. We get lots of e-mail testimonies sent to our offices, but what has surprised me the most is how many people I run into in public places who are subscribers. This, too, has been an example of seeing where God is at work.

Sometimes we assume God is not working when he is actually working in the most unlikely of places. Here are several stories, many quite humorous, of how God is using TGIF to minister to people in all walks of life.

THE MAN FROM BRAZIL

When God begins to use you in the lives of others, sometimes the responses of those you minister to can be unusual. Such was the case when my staff forwarded a message to me from a man named Joel from Brazil. The message basically said something like this: *I am planning to move to Cumming, Georgia, in order to learn from Os Hillman. I wish to rent an apartment near him. Please help make arrangements for me.* If you received a message like that from a perfect stranger, what would you do?

My staff quickly responded and discouraged the man from making such arrangements, and we said we could not assist such a request. Time went by, and we received a few more e-mails from him. Then, one day in December 2014, we learned that Joel had arrived in my hometown, was renting a room, and bought a bicycle to get around. We were shocked and concerned. Who was this guy?

He requested a meeting with me, but I had travel plans for the next week and could not meet with him. (By the way, did I mention that Joel did not speak English?) We all concluded this guy was a real nutcase; either that, or he had the faith and boldness of an apostle. A week later, a friend of mine was staying with me. I told him about Joel and he said, "Let's meet this man. This is an amazing thing he has done. We need to see if he is for real."

I had my assistant arrange a meeting, and we went by his hotel to pick him up. He spoke a little broken English, so communicating was difficult. He told us a little of his story. He was in his thirties and was a former professional poker player in Brazil—that explained his gambling nature. He came to Christ and left that profession and began reading TGIF. God did a deep work in his life, and he wanted to meet me because of the impact TGIF had on his life.

Over the next week, I met with Joel and got to know him better. Then the most unusual thing happened. The Holy Spirit spoke to me. *Let Joel live with you.*

My response was, *Are you kidding me?*

I wrestled for several days with this instruction, but finally yielded. For the next several months, God had me serve Joel. I took him to get a driver's license, I helped him get a car, I helped him learn English, and had him, participate in our Tuesday night men's group. Our guys embraced him, and he began to grow in his faith. Joel stayed with me for about two months, then eventually returned to Brazil. He now wants to take some of what he learned from me back to Brazil.

THE NIGERIANS

We have a small staff. We used to have an office but decided we could work virtually with each member working out of his home. So my office is in my home. For years, my home address was on our website. I happened to be home when I heard my doorbell ring. I came to the door and was surprised to see five strangers standing about fifteen feet from my door in my front yard. It was odd to me that they were standing that far away from the front door instead of at the door.

I hesitantly opened the door and a man approached me with his hand extended with his phone in it. He asked, "Does the man who writes these devotionals live here?" I could see he was referring to the devotional I had written.

"Yes," I replied. "I am Os Hillman, the writer of these messages."

He quickly responded by saying what a pleasure it was to meet me. He thought he was coming to our Marketplace Leader offices and did not know it was a home. He and his friends were from Nigeria and wanted to come and buy some resources from us to take back to Nigeria. I realized God had brought them to meet me, and so I invited them in. They spent about an hour visiting our resource area, and I learned about their ministry as well. One of them was a pastor in Nigeria, and one of them was his son who lived in the Atlanta area.

The Ticket Agent

One day I was checking in for a flight in the Atlanta airport. A man walked up to me as I was standing at the ticket counter and said, "Os, how are you?" I had met this man a few months earlier; he was the Atlanta airport chaplain. He went on to say: "You put me on the subscription list, and I have thoroughly enjoyed your messages. They have really encouraged me."

We exchanged our greetings and then he left. I turned to the ticket agent at the counter who was checking me in and she said, "I, too, enjoy TGIF every day. Thank you for what you do." I walked away thinking, *God, you are working in so many areas we cannot see. Thank you for letting me see.*

On another occasion, I was traveling through the Minneapolis airport and my daughter and I were trying to find the rental car area. There was an information desk in the airport, so I inquired from the man at the desk about the location of the rental car area. He responded by saying, "It's right over there, Os."

At first I wasn't sure what I heard, then my daughter said, "He just called you by your name!"

I turned back to the man. "How do you know my name?"

"I read you every day," he said. "Thank you for what you do."

An Executive Gets Relocated

Several years ago, I was attending a local church where the pastor and I were good friends. There was an avid reader in St. Louis who was an executive being relocated to the Atlanta area. He looked up churches in the Yellow Pages to see about attending a local church near his office and new residence. He found a church that seemed interesting to him, attended a few services, and called to meet with the pastor.

During their lunch meeting, he told the pastor about a devotional that had a big impact on his life, called TGIF, written by a man named Os Hillman. The pastor, a bit shocked by his statement, smiled at the executive and said, "Os is a member of our church! In fact, Os leads a lunchtime Bible study that is directly across the street from your place of work." The executive nearly fell out of his chair! He started attending the meetings.

OTHER GOD ENCOUNTERS

One of my best friend's wife, Sharon, is a banker. They often had a devotional time in their bank among the Christian employees. One day a woman started to share a spiritual truth she learned by "reading a devotional called TGIF by Os Hillman." When Sharon heard her say those words, she matter-of-factly responded, "I know Os Hillman. He is good friends with my husband. Danny plays golf with him every week." The woman was shocked.

Danny and I were playing in a golf tournament in Macon, Georgia, one summer and had to check into a hotel. When I gave my ID to the woman behind the counter, she looked at my name and said, "Hmm, you remind me of a preacher I read by the same name. His devotional really helps me." Danny and I smiled at her. A few moments later she realized I was the writer, and she jumped up and down and turned around in a circle, exclaiming, "You've got to be kidding me! You are Os Hillman!" She ran around the counter and went to get another employee to tell her, "This is the man I always share the devotionals with you about."

Such encounters are an encouragement from the Lord to see how God is working in the lives of those in the trenches of everyday work. It is so gracious of God to let me see the firsthand fruit of serving the Lord in the marketplace.

I had a similar situation as above happen at Home Depot. I was returning a product to Home Depot and had to give my ID to the woman at the counter. She, too, made a similar statement as the hotel clerk: "Hmm, I read a devotional by a guy that has the same name." Again, a similar reaction came from this woman, although not quite as extreme as the hotel clerks.

Recently I walked into the golf shop where I play golf. The assistant pro told me, "You are not going to believe what happened with my wife this week. She was reading out loud a devotional to me. She said it was by a man named Os Hillman. I turned to her and said, 'Os Hillman? I know Os Hillman! He is a member of our club!' She was, needless to say, shocked." Later I gave him a signed pocket version of the TGIF book to give to his wife.

As things like this continued to happen, I became more aware of where God was working in the lives of his people and how he was encouraging me to know he was using me as well.

"Do You Write Some Kind of Devotional?"

In 2008, our ministry held a conference on the seven cultural mountains of greatest influence in society. These mountains include business, government, arts and entertainment, media, education, family, government, and religion. I invited Larry Poland, president of Master Media, to be one of our featured speakers for arts and entertainment. Larry has had a thirty-year-plus history of serving those in entertainment and media in Hollywood and New York. He shared a wonderful message on understanding God's activity in Hollywood.

I had not seen or talked to Larry for a few years after that, until I received a phone call from him. "Os, do you write some type of devotional?" he asked me.

"Yes, I do," I said. "Why do you ask?"

"Well, I've been working with a top executive at one of the major studios for many, many years. He began telling me about how much your devotional has impacted his life, and wondered if I knew you. He asked if I could introduce you to him."

I called the man and visited with him by phone, and then visited him in his office on our next trip to Hollywood. God touched the studio executive deeply. We had subsequent meetings with him in his high-rise offices in Hollywood. This began a whole new focus for us in Hollywood that would take us back many times and even host our Change Agent training for those in the entertainment industry.

THE MAN FROM ENGLAND

One day I received a phone call from a former client of mine. We had not spoken for at least ten years. He left a voicemail message that went something like this: "Hello, Os. It has been a long time since we have spoken. I was recently in England and an old acquaintance told me he was reading some kind of devotional that you write, and he says it literally saved his life. He would like to talk to you."

I called the man back, and he began to tell me about a friend of his who was an influential person in England. He had gone through a difficult season in his life and said that my devotional was what got him through it. He wanted to talk to me. I called the man, and we visited over the phone. He told me a little of his story—it was quite humorous.

This man had been wealthy. His gardener had given him a photocopy of one of my books—he had photocopied every page of the book! This was not the devotional, but his wife later discovered my devotional and told him, "You must read this!" He began reading it, and it became a source of encouragement to get him through a life-threatening illness and financial crisis.

A few months later, this same man told me of his involvement with the Christian TV programing that he was overseeing and wanted me to consider creating a thirty-minute TV show for all of the UK.

I want to encourage you to be more aware of where God is working around you. Ask God to give you opportunities to share his love with those with whom you come into contact. One of the easiest ways to minister to people is to ask to pray for them when you hear of a need they have in their life.

The six stages of the Joseph calling are designed to usher you into the larger story of your life, which is the purpose of discovering, navigating, and fulfilling your destiny. Again, this should be a life that is filled with the activity of God and his presence being lived through you. God has a larger story for you. Are you ready to live in it?

18

THE TRUMPET CALL: KNOWING IS NOT ENOUGH— EXPERIENCE REQUIRED

It is not enough to teach people the principles of a walk with God. You cannot have just a Christian club. You must also engage them in the battle.

—J. Gunnar Olson[1]

The Christian's marketplace call must be a call of knowledge that is combined with power. Our six stages of the Joseph calling help us understand the processes by which God brings us to maturity. All of the leaders received a *trumpet call* that ushered them into the larger story of their life. God has something in mind for every believer, something for which we were brought to the earth to fulfill.

Much of life is spent in the not-so-glamorous day-to-day living of working, loving our families, and experiencing mundane life in the haphazardness of life. Oswald Chambers explains it this way:

What God calls us to cannot be definitely stated, because His call is simply to be His friend to accomplish His own purposes. Our real test is in truly believing that God knows what He desires. The things that happen do not happen by chance—they happen entirely by the decree of God. God is sovereignly working out His own purposes. ... Jesus never measured His life by how or where He was of the greatest use. God places His saints where they will bring the most glory to Him, and we are totally incapable of judging where that may be. ... It is ingrained in us that we have to do exceptional things for God—but we do not. We have to be exceptional in the ordinary things of life, and holy on the ordinary streets, among ordinary people—and this is not learned in five minutes.[2]

We often overestimate the extraordinary at the expense of the ordinary. Yet there is for some the extraordinary call that will impact the lives of many people and make a major contribution to the establishment of the kingdom of God on earth.

Everyone needs someone whom they can go to help them understand the deeper things of a journey with God. That person for me over the last twenty years has been Gunnar Olson. He became one of two spiritual fathers I am still in relationship with today. He became my marketplace spiritual father.

Gunnar Olson is the founder of the International Christian Chamber of Commerce that operates in more than ninety countries today. His story is a marketplace story of miracles. He chronicles his life story in a book called *Business Unlimited*, a must-read for any marketplace leader.[3]

Lately Gunnar has been challenging me to become aware of the trumpet call of God. What is it that God is asking of us, if we are to be an instrument to bring his glory on the earth? Are we willing to step into that call? Joshua had to step into the trumpet call and walk around Jericho to see its walls fall—that was a prophetic act of obedience. Would Moses accept the call to free the people of Israel from slavery and fulfill the trumpet call of his life? Would Gideon

> We often overestimate the extraordinary at the expense of the ordinary.

accept his role to destroy the idols of Israel? Would Jonah fulfill the assignment God had for him to go to Nineveh and deliver God's message to them? Would Paul accept his assignment to be an apostle to the Gentiles? We could go on and on with examples of those who were required to respond to their trumpet calls.

If you want to grow in your Christian life, then find people who are more mature and have much more life experience with God than you. Hang out with them and learn all you can. Too many young people don't hunger enough to do whatever it takes to grow into mature believers. I would often travel across the world to just spend an hour or two with Gunnar. He made such rich deposits in my life—I can never repay him for what he has sown into me.

A second man who made rich deposits in my life was Jim Mezick. I have known Jim and his wife, Genie, since I was thirteen years old. He was the catalyst to bring me to the Lord when I was twenty-two years old. He is a retired pastor now in his eighties, and we still talk with each other weekly. He is my spiritual father, while Gunnar is my marketplace spiritual father. Both of these men played critical roles at key times in my life. God often places people in our lives to help us move to the next stage of our spiritual maturity.

When Elisha went to serve Elijah, he left everything in order to follow him. Elisha killed his oxen so that he had nothing to fall back on. He was all in! Gunnar often said to me, "You must manifest the presence of God in the area of your calling." That has always been a challenging statement for me. The truth is that most of us struggle to experience this in our work, yet I have seen how Gunnar has experienced this repeatedly. I have experienced this as well, and I am trusting God to see much more of his presence manifested in my call before I am called home.

> It is not enough for us to know the Scriptures; we must experience them.

It is not enough for us to know the Scriptures; we must experience them. Knowledge without power is an exercise in futility. We cannot live based on knowledge; we must experience the reality of a living God. Paul said it well when he wrote, "My message and my preaching were not with wise and persuasive words, but with a demonstration of the Spirit's power, so that your faith might not rest on human wisdom, but on God's power" (1 Corinthians 2:4–5).

People are not attracted to what you know; they are attracted to what you live out in your day-to-day life. They want to see something that cannot be explained other than by the power of God working in an individual's life. They must be attracted to the God who lives within you. They need to see the reality of that relationship in us, and they need to experience the power for themselves.

"I Have a Brain Tumor!"

A friend of mine who leads a ministry that I served on the board of is a marketplace leader and a successful entrepreneur. One day I got a text message from him that read, *I think I have a brain tumor!* You can imagine my shock to receive that. I immediately called my friend to find out what was going on.

"I have had a horrible pain in the top of my head for two weeks," he explained. "I cannot turn my head without pain. I went to the doctor and he said that I could have one of three things, all of which are serious, including a possible brain tumor. He told me I needed to get tests done immediately."

I told my friend that we needed to bring our team of intercessors together over the phone to pray for him. His response was, "Oh, you don't have to do that. I don't want to bring attention to myself on this."

"Get out of your false humility and pride!" I told him. "We are going to pray for you tomorrow!" The next day I had about seven intercessors join me on a call. We prayed for about an hour.

The following day, I received an excited voicemail: "You are not going to believe what has happened! Call me!"

I called him back, and he began to speak excitedly: "I woke up with no more pain in my head. I think I am healed!"

We monitored his condition for the next several weeks. The pain never returned. It has now been about three months since he had those symptoms, and he still is symptom-free. We believe God touched my friend. This is the normal Christian life.

I am the first to admit we don't always see such an immediate answer to prayer. However, this does not mean we should not be obedient to do what the Bible says we should do, and to pray over every situation and ask God for his help.

Watch and Wait

Watch and wait for the trumpet call of God. When the signs appear, then step into it. Allow God to use you to be an instrument to manifest his presence into that specific situation. When you do, your life will never be the same again.

What does God want to do in the last chapter of his great story? What role do you and I play? The prophet Joel speaks of this as he describes a day that is coming when marketplace people will be used as a great army to bring many into the kingdom of God:

> Proclaim this among the nations:
>   Prepare for war!
> Rouse the warriors!
>   Let all the fighting men draw near and attack.
> Beat your plowshares into swords
>   and your pruning hooks into spears.
> Let the weakling say,
>   "I am strong!"
> Come quickly, all you nations from every side,
>   and assemble there.
> Bring down your warriors, LORD!
> (Joel 3:9–11)

And Micah tells us the people whom God will use in the last days are those who have understood the pain of the deeper call, the Joseph calling. God is going to use those who walk with a limp, those who have wrestled with him and prevailed:

> "In that day," declares the LORD,
>> "I will gather the lame;
>>> I will assemble the exiles
>>> and those I have brought to grief.
>> I will make the lame my remnant,
>>> those driven away a strong nation.
>> The LORD will rule over them in Mount Zion
>>> from that day and forever."
> (Micah 4:6–7)

It is not business as usual in our nation and the world today. We must be as the people of Issachar, who understood the signs of the times (1 Chronicles 12:32). In our day and hour, God said he was going to shake all that was not founded upon his name:

> See to it that you do not refuse him who speaks. If they did not escape when they refused him who warned them on earth, how much less will we, if we turn away from him who warns us from heaven? At that time his voice shook the earth, but now he has promised, "Once more I will shake not only the earth but also the heavens." The words "once more" indicate the removing of what can be shaken— that is, created things—so that what cannot be shaken may remain.
>
> Therefore, since we are receiving a kingdom that cannot be shaken, let us be thankful, and so worship God acceptably with reverence and awe, for our "God is a consuming fire." (Hebrews 12:25–29)

In this day and hour, we need to have confidence that God can fulfill his purposes if we make ourselves available to him for this season: "The one who calls you is faithful, and he will do it" (2 Thessalonians 5:24).

Joseph was a man to whom God revealed the signs of his time and what he was to do. He was even called to warn an ungodly king of what was coming because God cared for the people. God gave Joseph a plan that would save the nation of Egypt, as well as that of Israel, from starvation. That is how God works. He speaks to someone he can use to accomplish his purposes on the earth.

How do we change the direction America is taking today? It begins with God's people seeking God like never before. God said, "If my people, who are called by my name, will humble themselves and pray and seek my face and turn from their wicked ways, then I will hear from heaven, and I will forgive their sin and will heal their land" (2 Chronicles 7:14). This is an invitation to wrestle with God, to seek his face, and to seek to know his will for this day and hour.

Josephs will play a key role in the last days when the foundations are being shaken. Many are in their pits, while some have not yet entered them. Those who have been trained in the Joseph calling process will mentor those who are yet to begin their journey. The shaking of the nations and the financial markets will birth many new Josephs in this day and hour. Are you ready to be God's Joseph in this season?

> If you extend your soul to the hungry
> And satisfy the afflicted soul,
> Then your light shall dawn in the darkness,
> And your darkness shall be as the noonday.
> The LORD will guide you continually,
> And satisfy your soul in drought,
> And strengthen your bones;
> You shall be like a watered garden,

And like a spring of water, whose waters do not fail.
Those from among you
Shall build the old waste places;
Shall raise up the foundations of many generations;
And you shall be called the Repairer of the Breach,
The Restorer of Streets to Dwell In.
(Isaiah 58:10–12 NKJV)

And again, hear the words from Joel:

Proclaim this among the nations:
"Prepare for war!
Wake up the mighty men,
Let all the men of war draw near,
Let them come up.
Beat your plowshares into swords
And your pruning hooks into spears;
Let the weak say, 'I am strong.'"
Assemble and come, all you nations,
And gather together all around.
Cause Your mighty ones to go down there, O LORD.
(Joel 3:9–12)

Amen! Knowing about God and his ways is not enough; experience is required. Has God called you into a Joseph calling? If so, it is through these six steps that you will learn to discover, navigate, and ultimately fulfill the call of God upon your life. Are you ready for your assignment?

IDENTIFYING YOUR SIX STAGES OF THE JOSEPH CALLING

Now it's your turn. Perhaps you recognize in your own life the six stages God has brought you through in order to fulfill your Joseph calling. Or perhaps you are in the midst of one of the stages right now. Whatever the case, it is my desire that you would think about your life and the stages you see God has taken you through, or that he is presently taking you through. List them here. Describe the circumstances and what you have learned in each stage.

1. Recruitment:

2. Character Development:

3. Isolation:

4. Cross:

5. Problem Solving:

6. Networking:

A SUMMARY
OF KEY TRUTHS

The Six Stages of Preparation for God's Call

Here are the six stages of a call from God that I found in the Scriptures:

1. Recruitment: God recruits the individual to the larger story of his or her life usually through a crisis event.

2. Character development: God takes the individual through a series of character tests designed to prepare him or her for leadership.

3. Isolation: God often isolates the leader to turn messes into messages.

4. Cross: God usually allows a graduate-level test that brings the leader to the end of himself or herself. This is often a betrayal by someone close to him or her.

5. Problem solving: like Jesus, God presents his leaders with a major problem he has brought them to the earth to solve.

6. Networks: God values unity through networks of people to model John 17:21–23, which is Jesus' prayer for his people to be one as he and the Father are one, so that the world might believe in him.

Review of Chapter Key Truths

- God often puts us through the experience and discipline of darkness to teach us to hear and obey him. We can then become his messengers as he births a message through our life experiences.

- God releases his blessing in proportion to the character we allow him to develop in us. God will totally ruin us and remake us at the same time.

- God doesn't measure timetables; he measures growth.

- God always takes you down before he takes you up. He allows you to be forsaken in order to usher you into a deeper relationship with himself. You must have the acclaim of God before you have the acclaim of others.

- So often our initial vision must go through a death process before it can become God's vision.

- The more faithful we are in using our gifts to serve others, the more God begins to elevate us.

- During your desert time, God gives you a message or a solution to a problem that he will use to serve others. It becomes your authority from which you minister to others.

- God turns our weaknesses into his strength once he deals with the core issues of our lives.

- Jesus is the only person who made plan A in his life; God turns our plan B and plan C into his plan A!

- You will never know you are a giant killer until a giant attacks you. Life is about facing the giants in our lives. Change agents rarely grow up thinking they want to be change agents; rather, they are drafted into a conflict, then a calling and the larger story of their lives.

- Sometimes God wants to see if we will serve others in the midst of our own pain. This becomes a source of healing for others and the catalyst that leads to our own freedom.

- Relational capital is sometimes as important as financial capital.

- Oswald Chambers said, "Jesus never measured His life by how or where He was of the greatest use. God places His saints where they will bring the most glory to Him, and we are totally incapable of judging where that may be."[1]

○ "God uses enlarged trials to produce enlarged saints so he can put them in enlarged places!"[2] Every call from God is extraordinary; however, not every call is high profile. We may not affect the masses, but we are all called to a unique assignment from God.

○ Those who fulfill the larger story of their lives are rarely looking to do just that; it happens when a crisis takes place. The crisis becomes the front door to the larger story of his or her life.

○ Sometimes we must get to a deep level of pain and disappointment in order to motivate us toward real change. The pain to remain the same must exceed the pain to change. We don't want just a habit change; we want a real transformational nature change.

○ Some things are only discovered by the desperate soul.

○ God often allows us to go low in order to go high with God.

○ Overcoming crisis always leads to elevation and greater spiritual authority.

○ Visions make leaders passionate; thorns keep them authentic.

○ The ways of God are often fraught with what we perceive as unfairness, crisis, isolation, and doubts on the road to leadership.

○ Sometimes the winds of adversity force us to adjust our sails to capture a different kind of wind.

○ The waiting period only adds to the authority that is given because of the waiting and the testing we endure. The waiting period actually creates a level of authority for us to carry out our assignment from God.

○ If God calls us into darkness so we can enter his presence, then that darkness will become an entry to new levels of relationship with a God who longs for fellowship with you and me. Networks are always necessary to create change in culture.

○ Those God uses to significantly impact the kingdom are often required to experience the deepest level of adversity, which will light the torch to illuminate the often-dark passageways for those yet to follow.

○ We might be able to put two nails into our own cross, but it always takes someone else to drive in the third one.

- We should never let the pain of the past steal God's vision for our future. Sometimes people live in their past.
- God gives us visions on the mountain but leads us into the valley to work out those visions.
- When we are forced into a battle we did not choose, this is the place of initiation to live for a cause greater than ourselves.
- The level of adversity corresponds to the level of call and the depth and width of the ministry and purpose God plans through your life.
- The farther we travel on our spiritual journey, the less responsive God seems to our requests for a pleasant life.
- One of the best ways to shipwreck our faith is to focus on things God is not doing instead of what he is doing.
- Sometimes subtraction comes before addition; dismantling before remantling.
- Don't let your circumstances change your faith; let your faith change your circumstances.
- When satan throws bricks at you, let God use them to build the kingdom by tapping into heaven and letting God solve the problem.
- I have concluded that most of us couldn't enter the larger story of our lives without the help of a significant disruption.
- If you are called to leadership, then you will be allowed to have someone close to you betray you to see if you are willing to wash the feet of your Judas.
- When God thinks of you, there is something he has in mind that you alone are uniquely qualified to do for God.
- God often puts us through the experience and discipline of darkness to teach us to hear and obey him. We can then become his messengers as he births a message through our life experiences.
- It is not enough for us to know the Scriptures; we must experience them.
- God often turns our messes into messages and makes us his messengers!

NOTES

Chapter 1

1 Edward Burke, from his "Speech on Mr. Fox's East India Bill," December 1, 1783, available at http://www.conservativeforum.org/authquot.asp?ID=254.

Chapter 2

1 Reputed to have been said by Mark Twain. See http://quoteinvestigator.com /2016/06/22/why/.

2 Oswald Chambers, *My Utmost for His Highest* (Uhrichsville, OH: Barbour, 2000), September 29.

3 Ibid.

4 Henry Blackaby, *Experiencing God: Knowing and Doing the Will of God* (Nashville, TN: Broadman & Holman Publishers, 1998), back cover.

Chapter 3

1 Lou Holtz, available at http://www.brainyquote.com/quotes/authors/l/lou _holtz.html.

2 Anonymous, quoted in Henry Blackaby and Tom Blackaby, *The Man God Uses* (Nashville, TN: Lifeway Christian Resources, 1998), n. p.

3 R. T. Kendall, *The Anointing: Yesterday, Today, and Tomorrow* (Lake Mary, FL: Charisma House, 2003), 12.

4 Ibid.

5 Oswald Chambers, *Not Knowing Where* (Grand Rapids, MI: Discovery House, 1989), quoted in Oswald Chambers, *Faith: A Holy Walk*, ed. Julie Ackerman Link (Grand Rapids, MI: Discovery House, 2011), Google e-book.

6 Einar Billing, *Our Calling* (Philadelphia, PA: Fortress Press, 1964), 30.

7 Chambers, *My Utmost for His Highest*, September 12.

Chapter 4

1 https://www.brainyquote.com/quotes/quotes/m/martinluth297522.html.

Chapter 5

1 www.forbes.com/sites/kevinkruse/2012/10/16/quotes-on-leadership/.

Chapter 6

1 www.quotecounterquote.com/2011/07/i-dream-things-that-never-were-and -say.html.

2 Oswald Chambers, *Not Knowing Whither: The Steps of Abraham's Faith* (Grand Rapids, MI: Discovery House, 2015), Google e-book.

3 Oswald Chambers, *Utmost: Classic Readings and Prayers from Oswald Chambers* (Nashville, TN: Discovery House, 2013), January 19.
4 Chambers, *My Utmost for His Highest*, accessed April 12, 2010, http://utmost.org.
5 Larry Crabb, *Shattered Dreams: God's Unexpected Path to Joy* (Colorado Springs, CO: WaterBrook Press, 2010), 78.
6 Bruce Wilkinson, *Secrets of the Vine* (Sisters, OR: Multnomah, 2010), 76.
7 C. S. Lewis, *Mere Christianity* (New York: Macmillan, 1952), 106.
8 Chambers, *My Utmost for His Highest*, accessed March 7, 2011, http://utmost.org.

Chapter 7

1 https://en.wikipedia.org/wiki/James_Stockdale.

Chapter 8

1 C. S. Lewis, *Mere Christianity* (New York: Harper Collins, 2001), 199.
2 Rick Warren, *The Purpose-Driven Life* (Grand Rapids, MI: Zondervan, 2002), n. p.
3 "Martin Luther," *Christianity Today*, http://www.christianitytoday.com/history /people/theologians/martin-luther.html.
4 Wikipedia contributors, "Martin Luther King Jr.," *Wikipedia*, http://en .wikipedia.org/wiki/Martin_Luther_King,_Jr.
5 Chambers, *Utmost*, Day 1.
6 C. S. Lewis, *The Problem of Pain* (New York: Macmillan, 1962), 93.

Chapter 9

1 Joseph Garlington, spoken at the Heartbeat International Conference in 2011, available at http://www.lifenews.com/2011/05/19/heartbeat-international -conference-marks-40th-anniversary/.
2 C. S. Lewis, *The Quotable Lewis*, ed. Jerry Root (Wheaton, IL: Tyndale House, 2012), 28.
3 Crabb, *Shattered Dreams*, n. p.
4 Henry Ford, BrainyQuote, https://www.brainyquote.com/quotes/quotes/h /henryford121339.html.
5 Graham Cooke, "The Act of Thinking Powerfully," Christian Healing Ministries, Summer 2014, https://www.christianhealingmin.org/index.php?option =com_content&view=article&id=670:the-art-of-thinking-powerfully&catid =214&Itemid=459.
6 Sara Blakely, interview with Wolf Blitzer, CNN, n.d.; a similar quote can be found at "75 Empowering Sara Blakely Quotes," Addicted2Success, http:// addicted2success.com/quotes/75-empowering-sara-blakely-quotes.
7 Quoted in *Streams in the Desert*, ed. L. B. Cowman (Grand Rapids: Zondervan, 1997), October 12.
8 Gordon Dalbey, *The Lion Speaks* (Nashville, TN: Thomas Nelson Inc., 2003), 7.

9   Steve Lentz, *It Was Never about the Ketchup* (New York: Morgan James Publishing, 2007), 47.
10 Quoted in Cowman, *Streams in the Desert*, May 8, 2010.

Chapter 10

1   Margaret Wheatley, *Finding Our Way* (Oakland, CA: Berrett-Koehler Publishers, 2005), 262.
2   Charles Swindoll, *Great Lives: David* (Nashville: Thomas Nelson Publishers, 1997), 73.
3   Lewis, *The Problem of Pain*, n. p.
4   Quoted in Cowan, *Streams in the Desert*, December 20.

Chapter 11

1   Jim Caviezel, reported by Kellie Hwang, *The Daily*, February 24, 2005, available at http://www.dailyuw.com/news/article_d4181234-009e-5ee0 -bfe8-47ec4795bdef.html.
2   Chambers, *My Utmost for His Highest*, March 24.
3   Jeanne Guyton, quoted in Gene Edwards, *100 Days in the Secret Place* (Shippensburg, PA: Destiny Image, 2002), 45.
4   Chambers, *My Utmost for His Highest*, May 16.
5   Chambers, *My Utmost for His Highest*, December 9.
6   Quoted in Cowman, *Streams in the Desert*, September 21.
7   Oswald Chambers, *The Complete Works of Oswald Chambers*, ed. David McCasland (Grand Rapids, MI: Discovery House, 2000), 938.
8   Ibid.
9   Chambers, *My Utmost for His Highest*, January 15.
10 Michael Molinos, quoted in Edwards, *100 Days in the Secret Place*, 135.

Chapter 12

1   George Washington Carver, May 25, 1915, quoted in *George Washington Carver: In His Own Words*, ed. Gary Kremer (Columbia, Mo: University of Missouri Press, 1987), 1.
2   William Joseph Federer, *America's God and Country: Encyclopedia of Quotations* (Dallas: Amerisearch, 2000), 270.
3   Ibid.
4   Billy Graham, quoted in Gabe Lyons, *The Next Christians* (Wheaton, Il: Tyndale House Publishers), 8.

5   Federer, *America's God and Country*, 97.
6   Edmund Burke, "Quotations by Author," The Quotations Page, http://www .quotationspage.com/quotes/Edmund_Burke.
7   Nancy Alcorn, quoted in Jane Hamon, *The Deborah Company* (Shippensburg, PA: Destiny Image, 2011), n. p.
8   McCasland, *The Complete Works of Oswald Chambers*, 937.
9   Nelson Mandela, BrainyQuote, https://www.brainyquote.com/quotes /quotes/n/nelsonmand133378.html.

Chapter 13

1   Theodore Roosevelt, *The Man in the Arena: Selected Writings of Theodore Roosevelt* (New York: Forge Books, 2016), http://www.goodreads.com/quotes/198923-i-am-a-strong-individualist-by-personal-habit-inheritance-and.

2   Wikipedia contributors, "William Wilberforce," *Wikipedia* https://en.wikipedia.org/wiki/William_Wilberforce; "William Wilberforce," The Wilberforce School, http://www.wilberforceschool.org/william-wilberforce.

3   Richard Gathro, "William Wilberforce and His Circle of Friends," *Knowing & Doing*, C. S. Lewis Institute, http://www.cslewisinstitute.org/webfm_send/471.

4   Ibid.

5   Ibid.

6   James Davison Hunter, *To Change the World* (New York: Oxford University Press, 2010), 38.

Chapter 14

1   Samuel Smiles, cited in Brainy Quote, http://www.brainyquote.com/quotes/quotes/s/samuelsmil126255.html.

Chapter 15

1   Les Brown, https://www.brainyquote.com/quotes/quotes/l/lesbrown119176.html.

2   Os Hillman, *Change Agent* (Lake Mary, FL: Charisma Media, 2011), 116.

3   Os Hillman, interview of Colin Ferreira.

4   Paul Tournier, *Creative Suffering* (New York: Harper & Row Publishers, 1981), 2.

Chapter 16

1   Peter Hathaway Capstick, ed., Theodore Roosevelt, *Theodore Roosevelt on Bravery* (New York: Skyhorse Publishing, 2011).

2   Crabb, *Shattered Dreams*, 152.

Chapter 17

1   https://www.brainyquote.com/quotes/quotes/p/petermarsh158664.html

2   Henry T. Blackaby, *Experiencing God*, n. p.

3   Colin Ferreira, in discussion with the author.

Chapter 18

1   Gunnar Olson, received in a personal conversation with the author.

2   Chambers, *My Utmost for His Highest*, August 5 and August 10.

3   Gunnar Olson, *Business Unlimited* (Orebro, Sweden: International Christian Chamber of Commerce, 2002), n. p.

Appendix 2

1   Chambers, *My Utmost for His Highest*, September 29.

2   Blackaby and Blackaby, *The Man God Uses*, n. p.

ABOUT THE AUTHOR

Os Hillman is president of Marketplace Leaders, an organization whose mission is to be a voice and agent to inspire, teach, and connect Christian believers to resources and relationships in order to manifest the life of Christ in their workplace call for cultural influence. Formally an advertising agency owner, Os is now an internationally recognized speaker on the subject of faith at work and a business owner. He is the author of seventeen books and a daily e-mail devotional called TGIF: Today God Is First, which has thousands of readers in over a hundred nations. He hosts a national radio show, *Faith, Work, and Culture with Os Hillman*, and has been featured on CNBC and NBC, as well as the *LA Times* and the *New York Times*.

Os is also founder and president of Aslan Group Publishing, which provides a leading online "faith-at-work" Christian bookstore called TGIFbookstore.com to serve the needs of Christians in their workplace. He also speaks to and trains leaders around the world. Os and his wife, Pamela, have one adult daughter, and they currently reside in Atlanta.

Please visit his websites to learn more:

MarketplaceLeaders.org

TodayGodIsFirst.com

BecomeaChangeAgent.com

OTHER BOOKS
BY OS HILLMAN

Listening to the Father's Heart

TGIF: Today God Is First Devotional, Volume 1

TGIF: Today God Is First Devotional, Volume 2

Change Agent: How to Be the One Who Makes a Difference

*Experiencing the Father's Love: How to Live as Sons and
Daughters of Our Heavenly Father*

The 9 to 5 Window: How Faith Can Transform the Workplace

The Upside of Adversity: From the Pit to Greatness

Making Godly Decisions: How to Know and Do the Will of God

The Purposes of Money

Overcoming Hindrances to Fulfill Your Destiny

*Faith@Work Movement: What Every Pastor and
Church Leader Should Know*

TGIF: Small Group Bible Study

Faith & Work: Do They Mix?

Proven Strategies for Business Success

So You Want to Write a Book

To learn more about these books, visit TGIFbookstore.com.

Subscribe to Os Hillman's free
daily e-mail devotional at
TodayGodIsFirst.com.

Walk with other Josephs.
Join the Change Agent Network at
TheChangeAgentNetwork.com.

We have created a 12-week Bible study
you can download for free.
Visit **TheJosephCalling.com** to download this study.
Why not start a small group using this resource?

TheJosephCalling.com